SEEKING THE KINGDOM

Seeking the Kingdom

Richard Foster

Hodder & Stoughton

LONDON SYDNEY AUCKLAND

All Bible readings are from the Holy Bible,
New International Version, © 1973, 1978, 1984 by
International Bible Society, 1980 edition, 1987 impression,
published by Hodder & Stoughton, except where
otherwise indicated.

Book extracts are as follows:
Chapters 1, 2, 3, 6, 9, 13, 15, 16, 17, 20, 24, 30 from *Prayer* by
Richard J. Foster, © 1992, published by Hodder and Stoughton Ltd.
Chapters 4, 5, 10, 11, 12, 14, 22, 23, 25 from *Celebration of
Discipline* by Richard J. Foster, © 1989, published by Hodder and
Stoughton.
Chapters 7, 8, 18, 21, 29 from *Freedom of Simplicity* by Richard
J. Foster, © 1981, published by Triangle/SPCK (Great Britain).
Chapters 19, 26, 27, 28 from *Money, Sex and Power* by Richard J.
Foster, © 1985, published by Hodder and Stoughton.

Copyright © Richard J. Foster

First published in Great Britain in 1995

The right of Richard J. Foster to be identified as the Author of this
Work has been asserted by him in accordance with the Copyright,
Designs and Patents Act 1988.

The Bible quotations on pages 77 and 80 are from the *New
Revised Standard Version*, Collins Publishers, 1989

10 9 8 7 6 5 4 3 2 1

British Library Cataloguing in Publication Data
A record for this book is available from the British Library

ISBN 0 340 64262 9

Typeset by Hewer Text Composition Services, Edinburgh
Printed and bound in Great Britain by
Cox & Wyman Ltd, Reading, Berkshire

Hodder and Stoughton
A division of Hodder Headline PLC
338 Euston Road
London NW1 3BH

Contents

Using this book

To get the most from *20 Minutes with God* you will need to have ready a Bible, a notebook and pen.

At times the Reflection will take the form of a number of questions to consider; in other places there will be an exercise or meditation for you to try.

There will be some days where you will find it helpful to write down your response; spaces have been allowed in the book for this.

Some chapters end with a section *For further study*; these are optional and should only be attempted by those who have more than twenty minutes available.

SECTION 1

Moving Inward

Nothing is more crucial to our lives nor more central to the heart of God than the transformation of the human personality. Paul, that great advocate of human transformation, once spoke of being 'in travail until Christ be formed in you' (Gal. 4:19 RSV). And in another letter he says, 'those whom God foreknew them he predestined to be conformed to the image of his son' (Rom. 8:29).

We must see it as our highest, most holy task – this being formed and conformed and transformed into the likeness of Jesus Christ. Unfortunately there is an abysmal ignorance today about the most elemental spiritual ingredients involved in character formation. The following readings have been selected in the hope of helping you understand this process a little better so that you may 'grow in the grace and knowledge of our Lord and Saviour Jesus Christ' (II Peter 3:18 RSV).

1

What keeps us from praying?

Reading: Isaiah 43:1b–5

Fear not, for I have redeemed you;
  I have summoned you by name; you are mine.
When you pass through the waters,
  I will be with you;
and when you pass through the rivers,
  they will not sweep over you.
When you walk through the fire,
  you will not be burned;
  the flames will not set you ablaze.
For I am the Lord, your God,
  the Holy One of Israel, your Saviour;
I give Egypt for your ransom,
  Cush and Seba in your stead.
Since you are precious and honoured in my sight,
  and because I love you,
I will give men in exchange for you,
  and people in exchange for your life.
Do not be afraid, for I am with you;
  I will bring your children from the east
  and gather you from the west.

We today yearn for prayer and hide from prayer. We are attracted to it and repelled by it. We believe prayer is something we should do, even something we want to do; but it seems as if a chasm stands between us and actually praying. We experience the agony of prayerlessness.

We are not quite sure what holds us back. Of course we are busy with work and family obligations, but that is only a smoke screen. Our busyness seldom keeps us from eating or sleeping or making love. No, there is something deeper, more profound keeping us in check. In reality, there are any number of 'somethings' preventing us, all of which we will explore in due time. But for now there is one 'something' that needs immediate attention. It is the notion – almost universal among us modern high achievers – that we have to have everything 'just right' in order to pray. That is, before we can really pray, our lives need some fine tuning, or we need to know more about how to pray, or we need to study the philosophical questions surrounding prayer, or we need to have a better grasp of the great traditions of prayer. And on it goes.

It isn't that these are wrong concerns or that there is never a time to deal with them. But we are starting from the wrong end of things – putting the cart before the horse. Our problem is that we assume prayer is something to master the way we master algebra or motor mechanics. That puts us in the 'on top' position, where we are competent and in control. But when praying we come 'underneath', where we calmly and deliberately surrender control and become incompetent. 'To pray', writes Emilie Griffin, 'means to be willing to be naive.'[1]

I used to think that I needed to get all my motives straightened out before I could pray, really pray. I would be in some prayer group, for example, and I would examine what I had just prayed and think to myself, 'How utterly foolish and self-centred; I can't pray this way!' And so I would determine never to pray again until my motives were pure. You understand, I did not want to be a hypocrite. I knew that God is holy and righteous. I knew that prayer is no magic incantation. I knew that I must not use God for my own ends. But the practical effect of all this internal soul-searching was to completely paralyse my ability to pray.

The truth of the matter is, we all come to prayer with a tangled mass of motives – altruistic *and* selfish, merciful *and* hateful, loving *and* bitter. Frankly, this side of eternity we will *never* unravel the good from the bad, the pure from the impure. But what I have come to see is that God is big enough to receive us with all our mixture. We do not have to be bright, or pure, or filled with faith, or anything. That is what grace means, and not only are we saved by grace, we live by it as well. And we pray by it.

Prayer

Reflection
What are the things that keep you from praying? You may find it helpful to write a list. There may be obvious factors, such as time and opportunity but also, looking deeper, less obvious hindrances such as your view of prayer or even your mental picture of God:

Bring your list before God in prayer, honestly and without self-justification, confessing what has kept you from
spending time with him.

End by re-reading the Isaiah passage at the beginning of
this section, hearing the words as if God is speaking them
to you personally, calling you by name because you are
precious in his sight.

2

The forgiveness of God

Reading: Luke 15:11–24

Jesus continued: 'There was a man who had two sons. The younger one said to his father, "Father, give me my share of the estate." So he divided his property between them.

'Not long after that, the younger son got together all he had, set off for a distant country and there squandered his wealth in wild living. After he had spent everything, there was a severe famine in that whole country, and he began to be in need. So he went and hired himself out to a citizen of that country, who sent him to his fields to feed pigs. He longed to fill his stomach with the pods that the pigs were eating, but no-one gave him anything.

'When he came to his senses, he said, "How many of my father's hired men have food to spare, and here I am starving to death! I will set out and go back to my father and say to him: Father, I have sinned against heaven and against you. I am no longer worthy to be called your son; make me like one of your hired men." So he got up and went to his father.

'But while he was still a long way off, his father saw him and was filled with compassion for him; he ran to his son, threw his arms around him and kissed him.

'The son said to him, "Father, I have sinned against heaven and against you. I am no longer worthy to be called your son."

'But the father said to his servants, "Quick! Bring the

best robe and put it on him. Put a ring on his finger and sandals on his feet. Bring the fattened calf and kill it. Let's have a feast and celebrate. For this son of mine was dead and is alive again; he was lost and is found." So they began to celebrate.'

God never despises 'a broken and contrite heart,' says the Psalmist (Ps. 51:17 NRSV). But the real question for us in the modern world is how do we experience a contrite heart, a grieving, broken, sorrowing, repentant heart?

We begin by asking. I wish that did not sound so trite, for it is the deepest truth we can ever know about our turning towards God. *We* simply cannot make heart repentance happen. It is not something that we cause to come about by creating a certain kind of mood with a certain kind of atmosphere and a certain kind of music. It is a gift from God, pure and simple. But it is a gift that God loves to bestow upon all who ask.

And so with boldness and persistence we ask for contrite hearts. We ask for weeping, lamenting hearts. 'Lord,' we may pray, 'let me receive the gift of tears.' If at first heart sorrow does not come we keep asking, we keep seeking, we keep knocking.

Like the tax collector in Jesus' parable we plead, 'God, be merciful to me, a sinner!' (Luke 18:13 NRSV). Not just once, or now and again, but with every breath. The ancient liturgical refrain *Kyrie, Eleison* (Lord, have mercy), comes from this parable. So does the famous Jesus Prayer, 'Lord Jesus Christ, Son of God, have mercy on me, a sinner.' We join with the multitude of voices from all the ages, asking for the gift of repentance, the Prayer of Tears. At times our prayer may be reduced to a single word: 'Mercy!'

Second, we confess. We acknowledge our lack of faith, our distance, our hardheartedness. Before a loving and gracious Father we declare our sins without excuse or abridgement; unbelief and disunity, arrogance and self-sufficiency, and offences too personal to name and too many to mention. C. S. Lewis notes, 'The true Christian's nostril is to be continually attentive to the inner cesspool.'[1] Paul's shocking declaration 'Wretched man that I am!' is the cry of the mature Christian longing for the spirit of repentance (Rom. 7:24 NRSV).

We leave no space for excuses or extenuating circumstances; we say, 'By my own fault, my own most grievous fault', as the old confessional rite reads. And like the old rite, we 'confess these sins, and all those I cannot remember'. The seventeenth-century poet Phineas Fletcher writes:

Drop, drop, slow tears,
*   And bathe those beauteous feet,*
Which brought from heaven
*   The news and Prince of peace.*

Cease not, wet eyes,
*   His mercies to entreat;*
To cry for vengeance
*   Sin doth never cease.*

In your deep floods
*   Drown all my faults and fears;*
Nor let his eye
*   See sin, but through my tears.*[2]

Third, we receive. Our God who is faithful and just – and also full of mercy – *will* forgive and *will* cleanse (I John 1:9). Like the father of the prodigal, he rushes to us at the first sign of our turning towards home. He lavishes us with good gifts that we do not deserve and cannot earn.

Prayer

Reflection

Use a simple meditation by which you place yourself in the role of the prodigal son. If you haven't attempted this before, the key rule is to let the story unfold without attempting to question or analyse. You are living the story as an active participant, not as a passive observer:

First re-familiarise yourself with the events in the parable.

Close your eyes. Picture yourself as the prodigal, far from home, hungry and wretched. Picture your surroundings in as much detail as possible (if you are drawn to something other than pig-keeping, that is fine).

Begin the journey home, rehearsing what you will say to your father in your own words as you are walking along the road.

See the reunion with your father and receive his loving response.

Think back over the meditation, observing your feelings and reactions. Ask God if there is anything he wishes to say to you through this story.

3

The school of Gethsemane

Reading: Luke 22:39–46

Jesus went out as usual to the Mount of Olives, and his disciples followed him. On reaching the place, he said to them, 'Pray that you will not fall into temptation.' He withdrew about a stone's throw beyond them, knelt down and prayed, 'Father, if you are willing, take this cup from me; yet not my will, but yours be done.' An angel from heaven appeared to him and strengthened him. And being in anguish, he prayed more earnestly, and his sweat was like drops of blood falling to the ground.

When he rose from prayer and went back to the disciples, he found them asleep, exhausted from sorrow. 'Why are you sleeping?' he asked them. 'Get up and pray so that you will not fall into temptation.'

We learn the Prayer of Relinquishment in the school of Gethsemane. Gaze in adoring wonder at the scene. The solitary figure etched against gnarled olive trees. The bloodlike sweat falling to the ground. The human longing: 'Let this cup pass.' The final relinquishment: 'Not my will but yours be done' (NRSV). We do well to meditate often on this unparalleled expression of relinquishment.

Here we have the incarnate Son praying through his tears and not receiving what he asks. Jesus, you see, knew the burden of unanswered prayer. He really did want the cup to pass, and he asked that it would pass. 'If you are willing' was his questioning, his wondering. The Father's will was not yet absolutely clear to him. 'Is there any other way?' 'Can people be redeemed by some different means?' The answer – No! Andrew Murray writes, 'For our sins, he suffered beneath the burden of that unanswered prayer.'

Here we have the complete laying down of human will. The battle cry for us is, 'My will be done!' rather than, 'Thy will be done.' We have excellent reasons for the banner of self-will: 'Better for me than them to be in control.' 'Besides, I would use the power to such good ends.' But in the school of Gethsemane we learn to distrust whatever is of our own mind, thought and will, even though it is not directly sinful. Jesus shows us a more excellent way. The way of helplessness. The way of abandonment. The way of relinquishment. 'My will be done' is conquered by 'Not my will.'

Here we have the perfect flowing into the will of the Father. 'Your will be done' was Jesus' consuming concern. To applaud the will of God, to do the will of God, even to fight for the will of God is not difficult . . . until it comes at cross-purposes with our will. Then the lines are drawn, and debate begins, and the self-deception takes over. But in the school of Gethsemane we learn that 'my will, my way, my good' must yield to higher authority.

We must not, however, get the notion that all of this comes to us effortlessly. That would not even be desirable. Struggle is an essential feature of the Prayer of Relinquishment. Did you notice that Jesus asked repeatedly for the cup to pass? Make no mistake about it: he could have avoided the cross if he had so chosen. He had a free will and a genuine choice, and he freely chose to submit his will to the will of the Father.

It was no simple choice or quick fix. Jesus' prayer struggle – replete with bloody sweat – lasted long into the night. Relinquishment is no easy task.

All of the luminaries in Scripture struggled as well: Abraham as he relinquished his son, Isaac; Moses as he relinquished his understanding of how the deliverer of Israel should function; David as he relinquished the son given to him by Bathsheba; Mary as she relinquished control over her future; Paul as he relinquished his desire to be free of a debilitating 'thorn in the flesh'.

Struggle is important because the Prayer of Relinquishment is Christian prayer and not fatalism. We do not resign ourselves to fate. Catherine Marshall writes, 'Resignation is barren of faith in the love of God . . . Resignation lies down quietly in the dust of a universe from which God seems to have fled, and the door of Hope swings shut.'[1]

We are not locked into a preset, determinist future. Ours is an open, not a closed universe. We are 'co-labourers with God', as the Apostle Paul put it – working with God to determine the outcome of events. Therefore our prayer efforts are a genuine give and take, a true dialogue with God – and a true struggle.

Prayer

Reflection
In which areas of your life do you find it most difficult to say 'not my will but yours be done'?

Picture in your mind the things that you find hard to relinquish to God. It may be a person, a possession, your bank balance or some situation. Imagine you are holding them before God with clenched fists, unwilling to open up or let go. Slowly allow God to uncurl your fingers. Truly relinquish all to him, now and in the weeks, months and years to come.

4

The revolution of submission

Reading: John 13:2–14

*The evening meal was being served, and the devil had
already prompted Judas Iscariot, son of Simon, to betray
Jesus. Jesus knew that the Father had put all things under
his power, and that he had come from God and was
returning to God; so he got up from the meal, took off
his outer clothing, and wrapped a towel round his waist.
After that, he poured water into a basin and began to
wash his disciple's feet, drying them with the towel that
was wrapped round him.*

*He came to Simon Peter, who said to him, 'Lord, are
you going to wash my feet?'*

*Jesus replied. 'You do not realise now what I am
doing, but later you will understand.'*

'No,' said Peter, 'you shall never wash my feet.'

*Jesus answered, 'Unless I wash you, you have no part
with me.'*

*'Then Lord,' Simon Peter replied, 'not just my feet
but my hands and my head as well!'*

*Jesus answered, 'A person who has had a bath needs
only to wash his feet; his whole body is clean. And you
are clean, though not every one of you.' For he knew
who was going to betray him, and that was why he said
not every one was clean.*

*When he had finished washing their feet, he put on his
clothes and returned to his place. 'Do you understand
what I have done for you?' he asked them. 'You call me*

*"Teacher" and "Lord", and rightly so, for that is what
I am. Now that I, your Lord and Teacher, have washed
your feet, you also should wash one another's feet.'*

The most radical social teaching of Jesus was his total
reversal of the contemporary notion of greatness. Leadership is found in becoming the servant of all. Power is discovered in submission. The foremost symbol of this radical
servanthood is the cross. 'He [Jesus] humbled himself and
became obedient unto death, even death on a cross' (Phil.
2:8 RSV). But note this: Christ not only died a 'cross-death',
he lived a 'cross-life'. The way of the cross, the way of a
suffering servant was essential to his ministry. Jesus lived
the cross-life in submission to all human beings. He was
the servant of all. He flatly rejected the cultural 'givens' of
position and power when he said, 'You are not to be called
rabbi . . . Neither be called masters . . .' (Matt. 23:8–10
RSV). Jesus shattered the customs of his day when he lived
out the cross-life by taking women seriously and by being
willing to meet with children. He lived the cross-life when
he took a towel and washed the feet of his disciples. This
Jesus who easily could have called down a legion of angels
to his aid chose instead the cross-death of Calvary. Jesus'
life was the cross-life of submission and service. Jesus'
death was the cross-death of conquest by suffering.

It is impossible to overstate the revolutionary character
of Jesus' life and teaching at this point. It did away with
all the claims to privileged position and status. It called
into being a whole new order of leadership. The cross-life
of Jesus undermined all social orders based on power and
self-interest.

Jesus called his followers to live the cross-life. 'If any

man would come after me, let him deny himself and take up his cross and follow me' (Mark 8:34 RSV). He flatly told his disciples, 'If any one would be first, he must be last of all and servant of all' (Mark 9:35 RSV). When Jesus immortalised the principle of the cross-life by washing the disciples' feet, he added, 'I have given you an example, that you also should do as I have done to you' (John 13:15 RSV). The cross-life is the life of voluntary submission. The cross-life is the life of freely accepted servanthood.

Celebration of Discipline

Reflection

What are the implications of Jesus' call: 'If any want to become my followers, let them deny themselves and take up their cross and follow me' (NRSV)? What does it mean to live a 'cross-life'?

What would be the result if people followed the way of servanthood in: the church, in management-trade union relations, in world politics?

How could you 'wash the feet' of others today?

5

In search of silence

Reading: Isaiah 53:4–7

Surely he took up our infirmities
and carried our sorrows,
yet we considered him stricken by God,
smitten by him, and afflicted.
But he was pierced for our transgressions,
he was crushed for our iniquities:
the punishment that brought us peace was upon him,
and by his wounds we are healed.
We all, like sheep, have gone astray,
each of us has turned to his own way;
and the Lord has laid on him
the iniquity of us all.

He was oppressed and afflicted,
yet he did not open his mouth;
he was led like a lamb to the slaughter,
and as a sheep before her shearers is silent,
so he did not open his mouth.

In Ecclesiastes we read, 'To draw near to listen is better than to offer the sacrifice of fools' (Eccles. 5:1 RSV). The sacrifice of fools is humanly initiated religious talk. The preacher continues, 'Be not rash with your mouth, nor let your heart be hasty to utter a word before God, for God is in heaven, and you upon earth; therefore let your words be few' (Eccles. 5:2 RSV).

When Jesus took Peter, James, and John up to the mountain and was transfigured before them, Moses and Elijah appeared and carried on a coversation with Jesus. The Greek text goes on to say, 'And *answering*, Peter said to them . . . if you will I will make here three shelters . . .' (Matt. 17:4, [italics added]). That is so telling. No one was even speaking to Peter. He was offering the sacrifice of fools.

John Woolman's *Journal* contains a moving and tender account of learning control over the tongue. His words are so graphic that they are best quoted in full:

I went to meetings in an awful frame of mind, and endeavoured to be inwardly acquainted with the language of the true Shepherd. One day, being under a strong exercise of spirit, I stood up and said some words in a meeting; but not keeping close to the Divine opening, I said more than was required of me. Being soon sensible of my error, I was afflicted in mind some weeks, without any light or comfort, even to that degree that I could not take satisfaction in anything. I remembered God, and was troubled, and in the depth of my distress he had pity on me, and sent the Comforter. I then felt forgiveness for my offence; my mind became calm and quiet, and I was truly thankful to my gracious Redeemer for his mercies. About six weeks after this, feeling the spring of Divine love opened, and a concern to speak, I said a few words in a meeting, in which I found peace. Being thus humbled and disciplined under the cross, my understanding became more strengthened to distinguish the pure spirit which inwardly moves upon the heart and which taught me to wait in silence sometimes many weeks together, until I felt that rise which prepares the creature to stand like a trumpet, through which the Lord speaks to his flock.[1]

What a description of the learning process one goes through in the discipline of silence! Of particular significance was Woolman's increased ability from this experience to 'distinguish the pure spirit which inwardly moves upon the heart'.

One reason we can hardly bear to remain silent is that it makes us feel so helpless. We are so accustomed to relying upon words to manage and control others. If we are silent, who will take control? God will take control, but we will never let him take control until we trust him. Silence is intimately related to trust.

The tongue is our most powerful weapon of manipulation. A frantic stream of words flows from us because we are in a constant process of adjusting our public image. We fear so deeply what we think other people see in us that we talk in order to straighten out their understanding. If I have done some wrong thing (or even some right thing that I think you may misunderstand) and discover that you know about it, I will be very tempted to help you understand my action! Silence is one of the deepest disciplines of the Spirit simply because it puts the stopper on all self-justification.

One of the fruits of silence is the freedom to let God be our justifier. We don't need to straighten others out. There is a story of a medieval monk who was being unjustly accused of certain offences. One day he looked out his window and saw a dog biting and tearing on a rug that had been hung out to dry. As he watched, the Lord spoke to him saying, 'That is what is happening to your reputation. But if you will trust me, I will care for you – reputation and all.' Perhaps more than anything else, silence brings us to believe that God can care for us – 'reputation and all'.

Celebration of Discipline

Reflection

Experiment with entering into silence. Start by setting yourself a realistic target, such as five minutes of silence. First you will need to find a comfortable position. Next, focus on relaxing each part of your body. Tense all the muscles in your face, then let them relax. Do the same with each part of your body: neck, shoulders, back, arms, hands, legs, feet. You are now ready to begin your silence. If something distracts you or a thought enters your mind, acknowledge it and then return to the silence. Note, you are not trying to think of things to say to God, you are simply allowing him to fill you in the silence.

Afterwards, reflect on how easy or difficult you found it to be silent. How could you make this part of your prayer life?

For further study: Determine to live a day without excusing or justifying yourself. Let God be your justifier. Observe your own reactions and reflect on how important your self-image is to you.

6

Holy obedience

Reading: Hebrews 5:7–10

During the days of Jesus' life on earth, he offered up prayers and petitions with loud cries and tears to the one who could save him from death, and he was heard because of his reverent submission. Although he was a son, he learned obedience from what he suffered and, once made perfect, he became the source of eternal salvation for all who obey him and was designated by God to be high priest in the order of Melchizedek.

We respond to the heavenly overtures of God's love first through the Covenant of Holy Obedience. Without reservation we vow to follow the Father's faintest whisper. In utter devotion and total simplicity we promise to obey the voice of the true Shepherd. Thomas Kelly writes, 'There is a degree of holy and complete obedience and of joyful self-renunciation and of sensitive listening that is breath-taking.'[1]

I know that all this sounds so frighteningly absolute and final. How can we possibly fulfil such promises? Well, *we* cannot. The matter of obedience is God's business and not ours. We cannot do a single good act unless God first gives us the desire for it and then empowers us to do it. But that is just the point. God *is* giving you the desire – you would not be reading these words if the desire was not already bubbling up inside you. And he will never give the desire to do something that he will not also give the power to obey.

Besides, obedience is really not as burdensome as it seems at first blush. We are doing nothing more than falling head over heels in love with the everlasting Lover of our souls. 'Oh love that will not let me go', confesses the hymn writer George Matheson. We are responding in the only way we can to the invading, urging, inviting, persuading call of Eternal Love.

God, you see, rushes to us at the first hint of our openness. He is the hound of heaven baying relentlessly upon our track. And he places within us such an insatiable God hunger that absolutely nothing satisfies us except the genuine wholewheat Bread of Life.

Sometimes we are invaded to the depths by an overwhelming experience of the love of God. Walking down the streets of New York, D. L. Moody was so overcome by God's loving presence that he rushed to the home of a friend in order to have a room alone where, for two hours, wave after wave of God's ravishing love swept over him. At other times we experience such a flaming vision of light that we are for ever blind to all competing loyalties. In the centre of his greatest spiritual moment Blaise Pascal wrote the single word, 'Fire!' Still others have a visitation of such indescribable peace that they stand and walk and sit and lie in wordless adoration and submission and wonder and glory.

We emerge from such soul-shaking, love-invaded times forever changed. We have swung like a needle to the polestar of the Spirit. Never again will any ordinary goodness do. No half measures will suffice. We are consumed by a relentless, inexorable divine standard of holy obedience.

I have discovered that such God-intoxicating experiences are far more common than we might at first assume. However, it is possible that we have never had such a soul-shaking encounter; that is all right. Nothing is wrong with us. We can share in the joyous wonder of such flaming visions through the biographies and journals of the saints and the wonderful stories of countless unnamed, unheralded ordinary people. After all, these experiences are given for the encouragement of all the people of God, not just a few individuals.

Also, we can cultivate the habit of a Godward directed mind and heart. As we carry on the business of the day, inwardly we keep pressing in towards the Divine Centre. At every opportunity we place our mind before God with inward confessions and petitions: 'Mercy, Lord'; 'I love you, Jesus'; 'Show me your way today.' Even more, we descend with the mind into the heart and live in quiet wonder and adoration and praise.

Prayer

Reflection

Have you ever experienced a sense of God's love or peace? It may not have been spectacular or overwhelming, but it may have been nonetheless real. What effect, if any, did the experience have on you?

Bearing in mind that 'God rushes to us at the first hint of our openness', how can you weave prayer into your daily experience?

For further study: Read the biography of a Christian who had an unmistakable hold on the reality of God's love, e.g. Corrie Ten Boom, C. H. Spurgeon, Dietrich Bonhoeffer, Teresa of Avila.

7

Saying 'No'

Reading: Matthew 5:33–7

Again, you have heard that it was said to the people long ago, 'Do not break your oath, but keep the oaths you have made to the Lord.' But I tell you, Do not swear at all: either by heaven, for it is God's throne; or by the earth, for it is his footstool; or by Jerusalem, for it is the city of the Great King. And do not swear by your head, for you cannot make even one hair white or black. Simply let your 'Yes' be 'Yes', and your 'No', 'No'; anything beyond this comes from the evil one.

I still remember the rainy February morning inside a Washington, D.C., airport many years ago. Exhausted, I slumped into a chair to wait for my flight. As always, I had brought reading material in order to make good use of free moments. For the first time in my life I opened Thomas Kelly's *Testament of Devotion*.

Immediately, he caught my attention by describing perfectly my condition and the condition of so many I knew: 'We feel honestly the pull of many obligations and try to fulfil them all. And we are unhappy, uneasy, strained, oppressed, and fearful we shall be shallow.'[1] Yes, I had to confess I was in those words. To all who saw me I was confident and in command, but inwardly I was tired and scattered. Then my eyes came upon words of hope and promise. 'We have hints that there is a way of life vastly richer and deeper than all this hurried existence, a life of unhurried serenity and peace and power. If only we could slip over into that Centre!'[2] Instinctively, I knew that he was speaking of a reality beyond what I had known. Please understand me, I was not ungodly and irreverent, just the opposite. My problem was that I was so serious, so concerned to do what was right, that I felt compelled to respond to every call to service. And, after all, they were wonderful opportunities to minister in Christ's name.

Then came the sentence that was to prompt an inner revolution: 'We have seen and known some people who seem to have found this deep Centre of living, where the fretful calls of life are integrated, where No as well as Yes can be said with confidence.'[3] This ability to say Yes and No out of the divine Centre was foreign to me. I had always prayed over decisions, and yet I too often responded on the basis of whether or not the action would put me in a favourable light. To say Yes to pleas for help or opportunities to serve usually carried an aura of spirituality and sacrifice. I could say Yes easily, but I did not have the ability to say No. What would people think of me if I refused?

Alone, I sat in the airport watching the rain splatter against the window. Tears fell on my coat. It was a holy place, an altar, the chair where I sat. I was never to be the same. Quietly, I asked God to give me the ability to say No when it was right and good.

Back home, I was once again caught up into a flurry of activity. But I had made one decision – Friday nights were to be reserved for the family. It was a small decision at the time; nobody but I really knew about it. I had told the family in a casual, off-hand fashion; they did not know it was a covenant commitment, a crossroads decision. Nor did I, really. It just seemed the right thing to do, hardly what one would call a God-given directive.

But then the phone call came. It was a denominational executive. Would I be willing to speak to this group on Friday night? There it was, another wonderful opportunity. My response was casual, almost unconscious, 'Oh, no, I can't.' The reply was also casual, 'Oh, do you have another commitment?' I felt trapped. (In those days I did not know that I could quite legitimately say that I did indeed have a very important commitment.) Cautiously but purposefully, I answered simply, 'No', with no attempt to justify or explain my decision. There followed a long period of silence which seemed to last an eternity. I could almost feel the words, 'Where is your dedication?' travelling through the telephone wires. I knew I had made a decision that made me seem less spiritual to one for whom I genuinely cared. After a moment we shared a few pleasantries and then hung up; but as the phone hit the receiver, inwardly I shouted, 'Hallelujah.' I had yielded to the Centre. I had touched the margin of simplicity, and the effect was electrifying.

Freedom of Simplicity

Reflection

Have you on occasions found yourself saying 'Yes' when you wanted to say 'No'? Why is it so difficult to use this simple, two-letter word?

Examine the pattern and fabric your life. Which description fits it most closely: 'Uneasy, strained, oppressed and fearful' or 'A life of unhurried serenity and peace and power'? Ask God to give you the ability to say 'No' when it is right and good.

8

Contentment

Reading: 1 Timothy 6:6–10

But godliness with contentment is great gain. For we brought nothing into the world, and we can take nothing out of it. But if we have food and clothing, we will be content with that. People who want to get rich fall into temptation and a trap and into many foolish and harmful desires that plunge men into ruin and destruction. For the love of money is a root of all kinds of evil. Some people, eager for money, have wandered from the faith and pierced themselves with many griefs.

One of the most profound effects of inward simplicity is the rise of an amazing spirit of contentment. Gone is the need to strain and pull to get ahead. In rushes a glorious indifference to position, status or possession. Living out of this wonderful Centre causes all other concerns to fade into insignificance. So utterly immersed was St Paul in this reality that from a Roman prison he could write, 'I have learned, in whatever state I am, to be content' (Phil. 4:11 rsv). To be abased or to abound was a matter of indifference to him. Plenty and hunger, abundance and want were immaterial to this little Jew with the Titan soul. 'I can do all things through Christ who strengthens me', he said, and so he lived (Phil. 4:13, KJV).

How cleverly Paul turned the tables on all those who taught that 'godliness is a means of gain' by replying that 'there is great gain in godliness with contentment' (I Tim. 6:5,6 RSV). He saw that the problem with material gain is its inability to bring contentment. John D. Rockefeller was once asked how much money it would take to be really satisfied. He answered, 'Just a little bit more!' And that is precisely our problem – it always takes a little more; contentment always remains elusive.

But the wonderful thing about simplicity is its ability to give us contentment. Do you understand what a freedom this is? To live in contentment means we can opt out of the status race and the maddening pace that is its necessary partner. We can shout 'No!' to the insanity which chants, 'More, more, more!' We can rest contented in the gracious provision of God.

I still remember the day this reality struck me with unusual force. I was passing by some very expensive homes, and began pondering our perennial tendency to want something bigger, better, and more plush. At the same time, I was monitoring the rise of covetousness in my spirit as I admired those homes. I carried on a little inward dialogue. Was it possible, I wondered, to come to the place where you do not desire more house even if you can afford it? Couldn't you decide on a particular economic livability level and rest contented with that, even if your income exceeded it considerably? The response was swift: 'Oh yes! It is not necessary to always crave more. You *can* live contented with what you have, with no further desire to accumulate more.' I'm quite sure I have not attained this holy contentment, but from time to time I have known a measure of its liberating graces and have found it a wonderful resting-place.

Think of the misery that comes into our lives by our restless gnawing greed. We plunge ourselves into enormous debt and then take two and three jobs to stay afloat. We uproot our families with unnecessary moves just so we can have a more prestigious house. We grasp and grab and never have enough. And most destructive of all, our flashy cars and sports spectaculars and home swimming pools have a way of crowding out much interest in civil rights or inner-city poverty or the starved masses of India. Greed has a way of severing the cords of compassion. How clearly the Apostle Paul saw this when he warned that our lust for wealth causes us to fall into 'many senseless and hurtful desires that plunge men into ruin and destruction' (I Tim. 6:9 RSV).

But we do not need to be imprisoned to avarice. We can be ushered into a life of peace and serenity. With Paul we can say, 'If we have food and clothing, with these we shall be content' (I Tim. 6:8 RSV).

Freedom of Simplicity

Reflection

What was the secret of Paul's ability to be content in whatever state he found himself?

What are the areas in your life which exercise the tyranny of wanting more or better? House? Clothes? Hobby? Career? Would it be possible to reach a state where you didn't want more, even if it was available?

Can it sometimes be a God-given desire to want to improve our state?

9

If I died today

Reading: Philippians 1:21–6

*For me, to live is Christ and to die is gain. If I am to go
on living in the body, this will mean fruitful labour for
me. Yet what shall I choose? I do not know! I am torn
between the two: I desire to depart and be with Christ,
which is better by far; but it is more necessary for you
that I remain in the body. Convinced of this, I know
that I will remain, and I will continue with all of you
for your progress and joy in the faith, so that through
my being with you again your joy in Christ Jesus will
overflow on account of me.*

Strange as it may sound to modern ears, the contemplation
of one's own death is among the most time-honoured
approaches to personal transformation. In our day of
runaway narcissism it is a practice we would do well to
revive. What would happen if you were to die today? If
I were to die today? One of the most sobering insights
from such a meditation is the realisation that life would
continue right on without us – and quite well for that
matter. The sun would come up the next day. People

would go about their normal duties. Nothing of substance would be changed.

This is a hard reality for us who carry the illusion that the world revolves around our decisions. How could anything of importance happen without us there? How *dare* anything of importance happen without us there! You see, we are a little like the fly on the chariot wheel in *Aesop's Fables* who looked back and declared, 'My, what a dust storm I'm causing!'

A Lutheran pastor friend – the Reverend Bill Vaswig – and I once were discussing Galatians 2:19 and wondering what it means to be crucified with Christ. I mean, what are we actually talking about? Bill said, 'Let's pray the passage into each other.' I had wanted to keep the discussion at arm's length, but I gulped and said, 'All right, how do we do it?' 'I don't know exactly,' was Bill's response, 'but you go first!' So I went over to him, placed my hands on his head, and began to pray. I have no idea what I said beyond the hope that he would experience what it means to be crucified with Christ.

When I finished and sat down, Bill looked at me wide-eyed and whispered, 'It happened!' 'What happened?' I responded blankly. He proceeded to explain that as I began praying, he saw a vivid mental picture of his church with a funeral service going on inside. He could see everything clearly: the coffin with the lid open, the chancel, the high arching beams. But he was seeing it all from inside the coffin. It was his funeral! As the people, filled with sorrow, filed past the coffin, he tried to tell them that everything was okay, that he was fine, and that what was happening was good. They could not hear him; all they could see was a corpse and yet he was more alive than he had ever been.

His prayer for me had equally powerful results for we were bathed in the milieu of the Holy Spirit that day. Most important of all, we both entered into a deeper understanding of death to the self.

Prayer

Reflection

A revealing exercise is to write your own obituary! The idea may at first sound morbid, but it can be a positive experience in reassessing our priorities in life. Write your obituary as you would *like to be remembered*. What qualities or achievements would you like others to recall in you? Let your imagination have free rein and include the things you dream of doing in the future, however unlikely they may seem (e.g. climbing Ben Nevis at the age of seventy!).

Look back on what you have written and see how closely it resembles your pattern of life at present. Is there anything you want to ask God's help to change in your way of life?

10

Careful for nothing

Reading: Psalm 126:1–6

When the Lord brought back the captives to Zion,
we were like men who dreamed.
Our mouths were filled with laughter,
our tongues with songs of joy.
Then it was said among the nations,
'The Lord has done great things for them.'
The Lord has done great things for us,
and we are filled with joy.

Restore our fortunes, O Lord,
like streams in the Negev.
Those who sow in tears
will reap with songs of joy.
He who goes out weeping,
carrying seed to sow,
will return with songs of joy,
carrying sheaves with him.

The Apostle Paul calls us to 'Rejoice in the Lord always:
and again I say, Rejoice' (Phil. 4:4 KJV). But how are

we to do that? Paul continues, 'Have no anxiety about anything', or as the King James Version puts it, 'Be careful for nothing.' That is the negative side of rejoicing. The positive side is 'in everything by prayer and supplication with thanksgiving let your requests be made known to God.' And the result? 'The peace of God, which passes all understanding, will keep your hearts and minds in Christ Jesus' (Phil. 4:6,7 RSV).

Paul instructs us on how we can always rejoice, and his first word of counsel is to be 'full of care' for nothing. Jesus, of course, gives the same advice when he says, 'Do not be anxious about your life, what you shall eat or what you shall drink, nor about your body, what you shall put on' (Matt. 6:25 RSV). In both instances the same word is used, which we translate, 'anxious' or 'careful'. Christians are called to be free of care, but we find such a way foreign to us. We have been trained since we were two years old to be full of care. We shout to our children as they run to the school bus, 'Be careful', that is, be full of care.

The spirit of celebration will not be in us until we have learned to be 'careful for nothing'. And we will never have a carefree indifference to things until we trust God. This is why the Jubilee was such a crucial celebration in the Old Testament. No one would dare celebrate the Jubilee unless they had a deep trust in God's ability to provide for their needs.

When we trust God we are free to rely entirely upon him to provide what we need: 'By prayer and supplication with thanksgiving let your requests be made known to God.' Prayer is the means by which we move the arm of God; hence we can live in a spirit of carefree celebration.

Paul, however, does not end the matter there. Prayer and trust by themselves are not adequate to bring us joy. Paul proceeds to tell us to set our minds on all the things in life that are true, honourable, just, pure, lovely, and gracious (Phil. 4:8). God has established a created order full of excellent and good things, and it follows naturally that as we give our attention to those things we will be happy. That is God's appointed way to joy. If we think we will have joy only by praying and singing psalms, we will be disillusioned. But if we fill our lives with simple good things and constantly thank God for them, we will be joyful, that is, full of joy. And what about our problems? When we determine to dwell on the good and excellent things in life, we will be so full of those things that they will tend to swallow our problems.

The decision to set the mind on the higher things of life is an act of the will. That is why celebration is a discipline. It is not something that falls on our heads. It is the result of a consciously chosen way of thinking and living. When we choose this way, the healing and redemption in Christ will break into the inner recesses of our lives and relationships, and the inevitable result will be joy.

Celebration of Discipline

Reflection

Divide a piece of paper into two columns. On one side list things that renew and recreate you, on the other things that deaden and stifle you. The lists do not have to be things that are traditionally regarded as 'spiritual'; they might include singing, swimming in the sea, listening to Mozart or Dire Straits – whatever you wish.

Another way of looking at these two lists is to head them 'Things that bring me closer to God' and 'Things that draw me away from God'. We tend to downgrade those things that are regarded as secular, but God can be found and celebrated in all things that are good. Is it possible to choose a way of thinking and living that will be suffused by joy?

SECTION 2

Moving Upward

Intimacy with God is seldom high on the priority list of contemporary people, including contemporary Christian people. It somehow feels too romantic, too ethereal. We need something more hard-nosed, more solid. And yet, what could be closer to the core of our purpose for living than loving God?

This section of readings focuses on this wonderful life of divine intimacy. Throughout we are learning to develop, as Thomas à Kempis put it, 'a familiar friendship with Jesus'.

11

The purpose of meditation

Reading: Psalm 119:97–104

Oh, how I love your law!
I meditate on it all day long.
Your commands make me wiser than my enemies,
for they are ever with me.
I have more insight than all my teachers,
for I meditate on your statutes.
I have more understanding than the elders,
for I obey your precepts.
I have kept my feet from every evil path
so that I might obey your word.
I have not departed from your laws,
for you yourself have taught me.
How sweet are your words to my taste,
sweeter than honey to my mouth!
I gain understanding from your precepts;
therefore I hate every wrong path.

In meditation we are growing into what Thomas à Kempis calls 'a familiar friendship with Jesus'.[1] We are sinking down into the light and life of Christ and becoming

comfortable in that posture. The perpetual presence of
the Lord (omnipresence, as we say) moves from a theological dogma into a radiant reality. 'He walks with
me and he talks with me' ceases to be pious jargon
and instead becomes a straightforward description of
daily life.

Please understand me: I am not speaking of some
mushy, giddy, buddy-buddy relationship. All such sen-
timentality only betrays how little we know, how distant
we are from the Lord high and lifted up who is revealed to
us in scripture. Johns tells us in his Apocalypse that when
he saw the reigning Christ, he fell at his feet as though
dead, and so should we (Rev. 1:17). No, I am speaking of
a reality more akin to what the disciples felt in the upper
room when they experienced both intense intimacy and
awful reverence.

What happens in meditation is that we create the
emotional and spiritual space which allows Christ to
construct an inner sanctuary in the heart. The wonderful
verse 'I stand at the door and knock . . .' was originally
penned for believers, not unbelievers (Rev. 3:20). We
who have turned our lives over to Christ need to know
how very much he longs to eat with us, to commune with
us. He desires a perpetual Eucharistic feast in the inner
sanctuary of the heart. Meditation opens the door and,
although we are engaging in specific meditation exercises
at specific times, the aim is to bring this living reality into
all of life. It is a portable sanctuary that is brought into
all we are and do.

Inward fellowship of this kind transforms the inner
personality. We cannot burn the eternal flame of the
inner sanctuary and remain the same, for the Divine Fire
will consume everything that is impure. Our ever-present
Teacher will always be leading us into 'righteousness and
peace and joy in the Holy Spirit' (Rom. 14:17 RSV).
Everything that is foreign to his way we will have to
let go. No, not 'have to' but 'want to', for our desires
and aspirations will be more and more conformed to his

way. Increasingly, everything within us will swing like a needle to the polestar of the Spirit.

Celebration of Discipline

Reflection

The Palmist talks of God's promises being 'sweeter than honey to my mouth'. For centuries Christians have been meditating upon Scripture and savouring its goodness. Meditation is about drinking in Scripture, hearing God speak to you personally through his word. As Dietrich Bonhoeffer has said '. . . just as you do not analyse the words of someone you love, but accept them as they are said to you, accept the Word of Scripture and ponder it in your heart, as Mary did'.

Meditate upon the following promise, rolling it around like honey in your mouth until you have sucked all the sweetness from it: 'Come to me, all you who are weary and burdened, and I will give you rest. Take my yoke upon you and learn from me, for I am gentle and humble in heart, and you will find rest for your souls' (Matthew 11:28–9).

12

The book of nature

Reading: Psalm 8:3–9

When I consider your heavens,
*   the work of your fingers,*
the moon and the stars,
*   which you have set in place,*
what is man that you are mindful of him,
*   the son of man that you care for him?*
You made him a little lower than the heavenly beings
*   and crowned him with glory and honour*

You made him ruler over the works of your hands;
*   you put everything under his feet:*
all flocks and herds,
*   and the beasts of the field,*
the birds of the air,
*   and the fish of the sea,*
*   all that swim the paths of the seas.*

O Lord, our Lord,
*   how majestic is your name in all the earth!*

We now come to the least recognised but perhaps the most important field of study: the observation of reality

in things, events, and actions. The easiest place to begin
is with nature. It is not difficult to see that the created
order has many things to teach us.

Isaiah tells us that '. . . the mountains and the hills
before you shall break forth into singing, and all the
trees of the field shall clap their hands' (Isa. 55:12 RSV).
The handiwork of the Creator can speak to us and
teach us if we will listen. Martin Buber tells the story
of the rabbi who went to a pond every day at dawn to
learn 'the song with which the frogs praise God'.[1]

We begin the study of nature by paying attention. We
see flowers or birds. We observe them carefully and
prayerfully. André Gide describes the time when he
observed a moth being reborn from its chrysalis during
a classroom lecture. He was filled with wonder, awe, joy
at this metamorphosis, this resurrection. Enthusiastically,
he showed it to his professor who replied with a note of
disapproval, 'What! Didn't you know that a chrysalis is the
envelope of a butterfly? Every butterfly you see has come
out of a chrysalis. It's perfectly natural.' Disillusioned,
Gide wrote, 'Yes, indeed, I knew my *natural* history as
well, perhaps better than he . . . But because it was
natural, could he not see that it was marvellous? Poor
creature! From that day, I took a dislike to him and a
loathing to his lessons.'[2] Who wouldn't! Gide's professor
had only amassed information; he had not studied. And so
the first step in the study of nature is reverent observation.
A leaf can speak of order and variety, complexity and
symmetry. Evelyn Underhill writes, 'Gather yourself up,
as the exercises of recollection have taught you to do. Then
. . . stretch out by a distinct act of loving will towards one
of the myriad manifestations of life that surround you . . .
As to the object of contemplation, it matters little. From
Alp to insect, anything will do, provided that your attitude
be right.'[3]

The next step is to make friends with the flowers
and the trees and the little creatures that creep upon
the earth. Like the fabled Dr Doolittle, talk with the

animals. Of course, you can't really talk to each other . . . or can you? There is certainly a communication that goes beyond words, and often animals seem to respond to our friendship and compassion. I know this because I have experimented with it and so have some first-rate scientists, and we have found it to be true. Perhaps the stories of St Francis taming the wolf of Gubbio and preaching to the birds are not so far-fetched. Of this much we can be sure: if we love the creation, we will learn from it. In *The Brothers Karamazov* Dostoevski counsels, 'Love all God's creation, the whole and every grain of sand in it. Love every leaf, every ray of God's light. Love the animals, love the plants, love everything. If you love everything, you will perceive the divine mystery in things. Once you perceive it, you will begin to comprehend it better every day.'[4]

Celebration of Discipline

Reflection

Find a leaf, stone or some other natural object to study (it doesn't necessarily have to be beautiful or unusual). Hold it in the palm of your hand and use your sense of sight, touch and smell to become familiar with it. Ask yourself what it would feel like to *be* that object – i.e. does the stone feel strong, worn down, smooth and serviceable? Finally, end by asking God what he wants to say to you through this piece of his creation. Allow time to hear his voice.

For further study: One enjoyable way to study the Book of Nature is to go on a Reflective Walk. This simply involves taking a walk on your own in a quiet park or garden. Along the way, take time to study nature in leisurely detail. Ask God if there is anything he wants to teach you through what you see.

13

Adventure in adoration

Reading: Psalm 100:1–5
> Shout for joy to the Lord, all the earth.
>   Worship the Lord with gladness;
>   come before him with joyful songs.
> Know that the Lord is God.
>   It is he who made us, and we are his;
>   we are his people, the sheep of his pasture.
>
> Enter his gates with thanksgiving
>   and his courts with praise;
>   give thanks to him and praise his name.
> For the Lord is good and his love endures for ever;
>   his faithfulness continues through all generations.

I went to the annual meeting of a small group of writers in high spirits. The *esprit de corps* and tête-à-tête are always exhilarating. This particular year we were meeting at a lovely resort near the Canadian border. Quickly, however, I found myself withdrawing from the intellectual bantering. I did not fully understand the reasons for my inner seclusion. 'I am weary from a hectic travel schedule,'

I reasoned, 'and my spirit has grown sad, weighed down by the pains and sorrows of many. Perhaps a little solitude would solve the problem.' Deep within, however, I sensed the need for something more than mere solitude . . . but what?

The next day the early afternoon was free, and optional readings were scheduled for the late afternoon – a perfect time to be alone. Following lunch, I went on a solo hike near a lovely lake, thrilling at the infinite variety of blues and greens. Then, I drove to a nearby town and strolled about the shops, my anonymity allowing for solitude in the midst of many people.

It was time to return for the readings, yet somehow I sensed that what needed to happen within me was not complete. On the drive back I spied an obscure sign pointing to a nearby waterfall. I turned up the winding road that cut its way through lush woods and ended at the falls. The sun darted in and out of the trees in a playful game of tag as I explored the area.

Following the river downstream for perhaps an hour or so, I eventually found myself off all existing paths and far beyond tourists and day hikers. I picked my way around boulders and over fallen trees until I came upon a huge outcropping of rock that jutted into the river, causing it to form a twisted U-turn. With much ado I made my way up this elongated granite thumb, and for some time I simply revelled in the glory of the canyon above me and the surging waters below.

What happened next is difficult to put into words. With the roar of the river quickly swallowing up any cry my voice could make, I felt free to shout out my thanksgiving and praise to God. A spirit of adoration and celebration sprang up within me, and I started dancing to the tune of a heavenly drummer and singing words unknown to my conscious mind. I sang with my mind too – hymns and psalms springing up from distant memory as well as spiritual songs that cascaded down in impromptu splendour. Thanksgiving poured forth for all things great and small.

Praises joined with the river in joyous exaltation. It felt as if I was being invited to join, in my feeble way, in the ceaseless paean of praise that ascends before the throne of God.

In the beginning the experience was wholly effervescent, but in time the exuberance began to give way to a whispered, 'Holy! Holy! Holy!' Worship grew deeper, more fertile. I had begun by blessing the name of God and was finally reduced to breathing the name of God. Exaltation sank into adoration.

Quiet murmurings of reverence continued for some time. Then a listening stillness came over me that yielded needed instruction for the days ahead. By now the long shadows in the canyon signalled the end of the day. In utter silence I made my way back upstream, bowed in awe and adoration.

Prayer

Reflection

It is not always possible for us to withdraw to a place of solitude and beauty to worship God. Yet God is always close at hand, no matter where we are, and we can learn adoration right where we are. Take a few moments to become aware of your surroundings. Are there things around you that can lead you into thanksgiving to a loving Creator – air to breathe, colours to see, etc. Now, on a deeper, more profound level consider who God is in himself: his unswerving love, for example. Allow your meditation on the person of God to lead you to praise, and praise to lead you to adoration.

14

An inward stillness

Reading: Romans 8:5–10

Those who live according to the sinful nature have their minds set on what that nature desires; but those who live in accordance with the Spirit have their minds set on what the Spirit desires. The mind of sinful man is death, but the mind controlled by the Spirit is life and peace; the sinful mind is hostile to God. It does not submit to God's law, nor can it do so. Those controlled by the sinful nature cannot please God.

You, however, are controlled not by the sinful nature but by the Spirit, if the Spirit of God lives in you. And if anyone does not have the Spirit of Christ, he does not belong to Christ. But if Christ is in you, your body is dead because of sin, yet your spirit is alive because of righteousness.

One reason worship should be considered a Spiritual Discipline is because it is an ordered way of acting and living that sets us before God so he can transform us. Although we are only responding to the liberating touch of the Holy Spirit, there are divinely appointed avenues into this realm.

The first avenue into worship is to still all humanly initiated activity. The stilling of 'creaturely activity', as the patriarchs of the inner life called it, is not something to be confined to formal worship services, but is a lifestyle. It is to permeate the daily fabric of our lives. We are to live in a perpetual, inward, listening silence so that God is the source of our words and actions. If we are accustomed to carrying out the business of our lives in human strength and wisdom, we will do the same in gathered worship. If, however, we have cultivated the habit of allowing every conversation, every business transaction to be divinely prompted, that same sensitivity will flow into public worship. François Fénelon writes, 'Happy the soul which by a sincere self-renunciation, holds itself ceaselessly in the hands of its Creator, ready to do everything which he wishes; which never stops saying to itself a hundred times a day, "Lord, what wouldst thou that I should do?"'[1]

Does that sound impossible? The only reason we believe it to be far beyond us is that we do not understand Jesus as our present Teacher. When we have been under his tutelage for a time, we see how it is possible for every motion of our lives to have its root in God. We wake up in the morning and lie in bed quietly praising and worshipping the Lord. We tell him that we desire to live under his leadership and rule. Driving to work, we ask our Teacher, 'How are we doing?' Immediately our Mentor flashes before our mind that caustic remark we made to our spouse at breakfast, that shrug of disinterest we gave our children on the way out of the door. We realise we have been living in the flesh. There is confession, restoration, and a new humility.

We stop at the petrol station and sense a divine urging to get acquainted with the attendant, to see her as a person rather than an automaton. We drive on, rejoicing in our new insight into Spirit-initiated activity. And so it goes throughout our day: a prompting here or a drawing there, sometimes a bolting ahead or a lagging behind our Guide. Like a child taking first steps we are learning through success and failure, confident that we have a present Teacher who, through the Holy Spirit, will guide us into all truth. In this way we come to understand what Paul means when he instructs us to 'walk not according to the flesh but according to the Spirit' (Rom. 8:4 RSV).

Celebration of Discipline

Reflection

Stilling human activity and becoming receptive to Divine promptings is something that takes practice. Here is a simple exercise called 'Palms down, palms up' that can be used at the beginning of the day to attune yourself to God in the stillness.

Begin by adopting a comfortable position. Place your palms down as a symbol of your desire to hand all the concerns of the day over to God. Then let go of each of your concerns, saying something like: 'Lord, I give to you my anxiety about the phone call I have to make, I release my anger about what Shelley said to me, I surrender to you my worries about paying the bills this month . . .' With your hands palms down, release each concern into God's care.

Then turn your hands palms upwards as a sign of your desire to receive from God. 'Lord, I would like to receive your peace about that phone call, your love for Shelley, your reassurance, your joy . . .'

Spend the remaining time in silence, not asking for anything but simply allowing God's love to fill you.

For further study: Frank Laubach used to play what he called a 'Game with Minutes'. How many minutes a day can you spend in conscious communion with God? Start with just an hour and record how many minutes of that hour you felt you were in communion with God. Then experiment with how you fare in a whole day. Note this is meant to be a fun game, not a legalistic way to improve your standing with God.

15

The grateful centre

Reading: Psalm 121

I lift up my eyes to the hills –
  where does my help come from?
My help comes from the Lord,
  the Maker of heaven and earth.

He will not let your foot slip –
  he who watches over you will not slumber;
indeed, he who watches over Israel
  will neither slumber nor sleep.

The Lord watches over you –
  the Lord is your shade at your right hand;
the sun will not harm you by day,
  nor the moon by night.

The Lord will keep you from all harm –
  he will watch over your life;
the Lord will watch over your coming and going
  both now and for evermore.

Another stone to place across the waters of our narcissism
is what Sue Monk Kidd calls 'the grateful centre'.[1] Each

of us has such a centre in our lives – a time and a place where we were free of all the grasping and grabbing, all the pushing and shoving, all the disapproving and dissenting.

Let me describe my grateful centre to you. I was seven years old, and my parents were trying to move to the American West Coast. Our relative poverty, however, caught up with us, and we were forced to winter in the cabin of an uncle in the Rocky Mountains. The time was difficult for my parents, I am sure, but for me it was glory. For a city boy to be suddenly plopped down into a paradise of towering pines, rose quartz, and splashing streams – well, *paradise* is too mild a term. Even the primitive nature of the cabin – lighting by candle, heating by fireplace, plumbing by outhouse – only added to the adventure.

My brothers and I conquered many a granite fortress, finding arrowheads and secret hiding-places. When the winter snows came, we 'joined' Admiral Byrd on many a frozen expedition. For Christmas I helped Mum paint pine cones silver.

But my most vivid memory is of the fireplace. (I had never been around a fireplace before, all our heat heretofore having come from the coal furnace in our Nebraska home.) Every night I would pull out the bed that hid in the couch by day and climb under the heavy quilts, my head less than ten feet away from the crackling warmth. Night after night I would fall asleep, watching this strange yellow blaze that warmed us all. I was in my grateful centre.

Even today as an adult I can go back to that centre via the marvellous capacity of memory and there experience thanksgiving and gratitude to the God who gives every good gift. I am not trying to escape or retreat from the struggles and hardships of modern life, rather I am giving myself a point of reference from which to face those struggles and hardships.

You too have such a centre, I am sure. Go to it in your

imagination as often as you can and from that place allow whispered prayers of thanksgiving to flow forth.

Prayer

Reflection

Try and recall a time and place which is your 'grateful centre': a place that was restful, comforting, free of anxiety and good to be in. It may be a memory from your childhood or something which is more recent. When you have found your 'grateful centre', try to call it to mind in all its detail. Go there in your memory; see the light and shadow, hear the sounds, touch it and smell it. Stay there for as long as you wish and gradually allow yourself to express your thankfulness to God in simple words.

16

Sabbath prayer

Reading: Hebrews 4:4–10

For somewhere he has spoken about the seventh day in these words: 'And on the seventh day God rested from all his work.' And again in the passage above he says, 'They shall never enter my rest.'

It still remains that some will enter that rest, and those who formerly had the gospel preached to them did not go in, because of their disobedience. Therefore God again set a certain day, calling it Today, when a long time later he spoke through David, as was said before:

'Today, if you hear his voice,
do not harden your hearts.'

For if Joshua had given them rest, God would not have spoken later about another day. There remains, then, a Sabbath-rest for the people of God; for anyone who enters God's rest also rests from his own work, just as God did from his.

The Bible tells us that, after speaking all things into existence from ant to aardvark, and after breathing into the human species the breath of life, God rested. This 'resting of God' on the seventh day became the theological framework for the Sabbath regulation that summons us to rest in God. Now, before we dismiss this Old Testament Sabbath rule out of hand, it is important to see that there is a lot more behind it than the desire for a periodic breather. For instance, it has a way of tempering our gnawing need always to get ahead. If we ever want to know the degree to which we are enslaved by the passion to possess, all we have to do is observe the difficulty we have maintaining a Sabbath rhythm.

No teaching flowing out of the Sabbath principle is more important than the centrality of our resting in God. Instead of striving to make this or that happen, we learn to trust in a heavenly Father who loves to give. This does not promote inactivity, but it does promote dependent activity. No longer do we take things into our own hands. Rather, we place all things into divine hands and then act out of inner promptings.

You may recall that the children of Israel failed to enter God's rest even though he had brought them out of the land of Egypt, out of the house of bondage. Unable to trust in Yahweh, they rebelled and spent their remaining days wandering in the deserts of Sinai. With tragic finality God declared, 'They shall not enter my rest' (Heb. 4:3 NRSV).

Today we are invited into the Sabbath rest of God which the children of Israel failed to enter. 'It remains open for some to enter it', declares the writer to the Hebrews. The literal translation for 'pray always' is 'come to rest'. Through the Prayer of Rest we enter this intense stillness, this quiet alertness.

But how? How do we enter the Prayer of Rest? It is here that we face a serious dilemma. Our tendency is, on the one hand, to take firm control, or, on the other hand, to do absolutely nothing.

We most often begin by tackling prayer in the same way we have been taught to tackle every other problem – by hard work. We grit our teeth, intensify our will-power, and try, try, try. In reality this is a pagan concept of prayer in which we rouse the gods to action by our many incantations and vain repetitions.

Anthony Bloom tells the story of an elderly woman who had been working at prayer with all her might but without ever sensing God's presence. Wisely, the archbishop encouraged the old woman to go to her room each day and 'for fifteen minutes knit before the face of God, but I forbid you to say one word of prayer. You just knit and try to enjoy the peace of your room.'

The woman received this counsel, and at first her only thought was, 'Oh, how nice. I have fifteen minutes during which I can do nothing without being guilty!' In time, however, she began to enter the silence created by her knitting. Soon, she said, 'I perceived that this silence was not simply an absence of noise, but that the silence had substance. It was not absence of something but presence of something.' As she continued her daily knitting, she discovered that 'at the heart of the silence there was he who is all stillness, all peace, all poise.'[1] She had let go of her tight-fisted efforts to enter God's presence and, by doing so, discovered God's presence already there.

Prayer

Reflection
On the seventh day God rested and he has commanded that we should do the same. Why do you think the concept of Sabbath rest is so important that God included it in the Commandments?

In your life, is there a sense of balance of work and play, activity and rest? If not, which elements are dominant and how can you achieve a greater equilibrium?

Is your tendency in prayer to come at it through will-power and hard effort, or to sit back and be passive, expecting God to take over? Is there a middle way?

For further study: What are the possible consequences for our society of the erosion of a day of rest?

17

Jesus is praying for us

Reading: Hebrews 7:23–6

Now there have been many of those priests, since death prevented them from continuing in office; but because Jesus lives for ever, he has a permanent priesthood. Therefore he is able to save completely those who come to God through him, because he always lives to intercede for them.

Such a high priest meets our needs – one who is holy, blameless, pure, set apart from sinners, exalted above the heavens.

The wonderful news I am trying to explain is this: while we are full participants in the grace-filled work of prayer, the work of prayer does not depend upon us. We often pray in struggling, halting ways. Many times we have only fragmentary glimpses of the heavenly glory. We do not know what to pray. We do not know how to pray. Often our best prayers feel like inarticulate groans.

This is why the promise of scripture comes as such good news: 'The Spirit helps us in our weakness; for we do not know how to pray as we ought, but that very Spirit intercedes with sighs too deep for words. And God, who searches the heart, knows what is the mind of the Spirit, because the Spirit intercedes for the saints according to the will of God' (Rom. 8:26–7 NRSV).

Do you realise what a relief this is? The Holy Spirit of God, the third member of the Trinity, himself accompanies us in our prayers. When we stumble over our words, the Spirit straightens out the syntax. When we pray with muddy motives, the Spirit purifies the stream. When we see through a glass darkly, the Spirit adjusts and focuses what we are asking until it corresponds to the will of God.

The point is that we do not have to have everything perfect when we pray. The Spirit reshapes, refines and reinterprets our feeble, ego-driven prayers. We can rest in this work of the Spirit on our behalf.

But it gets even better. The writer to the Hebrews reminds us that Jesus Christ is our great High Priest, and, as you know, the function of the High Priest in ancient Israel was to intercede before God on behalf of the people (Heb. 7–9). Do we realise what this means? Today, as we carry on the activities of our lives, Jesus Christ is praying for us. Tonight, as we sleep through the long darkness, Jesus Christ is praying for us. Continual prayer is being offered at the throne of God on our behalf by none other than the eternal Son. You are being prayed for now. I am being prayed for now. We can rest in this work of the Son on our behalf.

But the best is yet to come. Hard as it may be for us to imagine, God is in everlasting communion with himself through our stumbling, bumbling prayers. P. T. Forsyth writes, 'When we speak to God it is really the God who lives in us speaking through us to himself . . . The dialogue of grace is really the monologue of the divine nature in self-communing love.'[1] How incredible! How beyond belief! 'We pray, and yet it is not we who pray, but a Greater who prays in us.'[2] One poet puts it this way:

They tell me, Lord, that when I seem
   To be in speech with you,
Since but one voice is heard, it's all a dream,
   One talker aping two.

Sometimes it is, yet not as they
   Conceive it. Rather, I
Seek in myself the things I hoped to say,
   But lo!, my wells are dry.

Then, seeing me empty, you forsake
   The listener's role and through
My dumb lips breathe and into utterance wake
   The thoughts I never knew.

And thus you neither need reply
   Nor can; thus, while we seem
Two talkers, thou art One forever, and I
   No dreamer, but thy dream.[3]

Prayer

Reflection
Examine the ideas about 'correct' or 'successful' prayer
you have inherited in the past. Do you feel that God will
not answer your prayers unless you get it right?

What are the implications of the Spirit interceding for us according to the will of God?

Meditate on the amazing promise of Hebrews 7:25: 'He is able to save completely those who come to God through him, because he always lives to intercede for them.'

The door to humility

Reading: Philippians 2:5–11

Your attitude should be the same as that of Jesus Christ:

Who, being in very nature God,
    did not consider equality with God something to be grasped,
but made himself nothing,
    taking the very nature of a servant,
    being made in human likeness.
And being found in appearance as a man,
    he humbled himself
    and became obedient to death – even death on a cross!
Therefore God exalted him to the highest place
    and gave him the name that is above every name,
that at the name of Jesus every knee should bow,
    in heaven and on earth and under the earth,
and every tongue confess that Jesus Christ is Lord,
    to the glory of God the Father.

Of all the theological virtues, humility is one of the most coveted. No one enjoys people who are consumed with themselves. Smug arrogance is always distasteful. Genuine humility, on the other hand, has a gentleness about it that is delightful. There is an unpretentiousness in true humility that all people appreciate.

But humility is as elusive as it is desirable. We all know that it can never be gained by seeking it. The more we pursue it the more distant it becomes. To think we have it is sure evidence that we don't. But there is a way for humility to come into the habit patterns of our lives. Holy obedience opens the door. It is a central means of God's grace to work humility into us. It is not hard to see how this can be. When the whole of our vision is filled with the Holy, petty selfishness is squeezed out. Perpetual God-consciousness of necessity eliminates self-consciousness. Thomas Kelly wrote, 'Humility rests upon a Holy blindedness, like the blindedness of him who looks steadily into the sun. For wherever he turns his eyes on earth, there he sees only the sun. The God-blinded soul sees naught of self, naught of personal degradation or of personal eminence, but only the Holy Will.'[1]

For the Christian, this comes as wonderful news. How many times we have longed to be free of our own self-conceit and domineering pride. What needless anguish we have borne simply because we were not noticed. We puff and strut to get a little attention, and later deplore our vanity. Wistfully we have seen the humility of others and ached to know its ease and freedom. How deeply we have desired to obey the word of Scripture to take on the mind of Christ, who though God the Son did not grasp for equality, but rather 'emptied himself, taking the form of a servant . . . And being found in human form he humbled himself and became obedient unto death, even death on a cross' (Phil. 2:7–8 RSV).

How wonderful now to see the connection between humility and obedience. Jesus 'humbled himself and became obedient'. There is a way into humility, and it is through holy obedience. The God-possessed soul knows only one purpose, one goal, one desire. God is not some figure in our field of vision, sometimes blurred, sometimes focused; he IS our vision. Our eye is single, our whole body is full of light. Selfishness cannot find a toehold.

Freedom of Simplicity

Reflection

What is the difference between false humility and genuine humility? How do you recognise someone who is truly humble?

In what ways did Jesus give us a model of humility?

Why is humility not achieved by a conscious effort? What is the connection between obedience and humility?

For further study: If it is not already your practice, try keeping a spiritual journal. It can be a source of great encouragement to look back over the years and see from what petty, self-centred depths God has brought us. Although we may still struggle and fail in obedience, we will begin to see that the issues we are concerned about are less superficial and more significant.

19

Mine or God's?

Reading: Matthew 19:16–22

Now a man came up to Jesus and asked, 'Teacher, what good thing must I do to get eternal life?'

'Why do you ask me about what is good?' Jesus replied. 'There is only One who is good. If you want to enter life, obey the commandments.'

'Which ones?' the man enquired.

Jesus replied, ' "Do not murder, do not commit adultery, do not steal, do not give false testimony, honour your father and mother", and "love your neighbour as yourself." '

'All these I have kept,' the young man said. 'What do I still lack?'

Jesus answered, 'If you want to be perfect, go, sell your possessions and give to the poor, and you will have treasure in heaven. Then come, follow me.'

When the young man heard this, he went away sad, because he had great wealth.

There is hardly anything more clear in the Bible than God's absolute right to property. To Job, God declares,

'Whatever is under the whole heaven is mine' (Job 41:11 RSV). To Moses, he says, 'All the earth is mine' (Exod. 19:5–6 RSV). And the Psalmist confesses, 'The earth is the Lord's and the fulness thereof' (Ps. 24:1)

We moderns find it difficult to identify with this teaching. Much of our training draws from the Roman view that ownership is a 'natural right'. Hence the very idea that anything or anyone can infringe upon our 'property rights' feels alien to our world view. This, coupled with our seemingly innate self-centredness, means that, for us, 'property rights' tend to take precedence over 'human rights'.

In the Bible, however, God's absolute rights as owner and our relative rights as stewards are unmistakably clear. As absolute owner, God put limits on the individual's ability to accumulate land or wealth. For example, a percentage of the produce of the land was to be given to the poor (Deut. 14:28–9). Every seventh year the land was to lie fallow, and whatever volunteer grain came up was for the needy, so that 'the poor of your people may eat' (Exod. 23:11 RSV). Every fiftieth year was to be a Jubilee year, in which all slaves were to be set free, all debts were to be cancelled, and all land was to return to its original owner. God's rationale for so violently upsetting everyone's economic apple carts was – very simply – that 'the land is mine' (Lev. 25:23 RSV).

God's ownership of all things actually enhances our relationship with him. When we know – truly know – that the earth is the Lord's, then property itself makes us more aware of God. For example, if we were staying in and caring for the vacation home of a famous actress, we would be reminded of her daily by the very fact of living in her home. A thousand things would bring her presence to mind. So it is in our relationship with God. The house we live in is his house, the car we drive is his car, the garden we plant is his garden. We are only temporary stewards of things that belong to Another.

Being aware of God's ownership can free us from a possessive and anxious spirit. After we have done what we can to care for those things that have been entrusted to us, we know that they are in bigger hands than ours. When John Wesley heard that his home had been destroyed by fire, he exclaimed, 'The Lord's house burned. One less responsibility for me!'

God's ownership of everything also changes the kind of question we ask in giving. Rather than, 'How much of my money should I give to God?' we learn to ask, 'How much of God's money should I keep for myself?' The difference between these two questions is of monumental proportions.

Money

Reflection

It is commonplace to talk about rights these days – workers' rights, women's rights, human rights, etc. As Christians, how are our relative rights tempered by God's absolute rights?

While it is easy to pay lip service to the idea of God's ownership of all we have (including ourselves), in practice it is much harder to live it out. As a symbol of your desire to live in this reality, make a list of all the things you usually assume to be yours – from the place where you live to your CD collection. Offer the list to God, asking him to free you from an excessive desire to hold on to what is his rather than yours.

20

Loving God

Reading: Hosea 11:1–4

When Israel was a child, I loved him,
   and out of Egypt I called my son.
But the more I called Israel,
   the further they went from me.
They sacrificed to the Baals
   and they burned incense to images.
It was I who taught Ephraim to walk,
   taking them by the arms;
but they did not realise
   it was I who healed them.
I led them with cords of human kindness,
   with ties of love;
I lifted the yoke from their neck
   and bent down to feed them.

Madame Guyon writes, 'Teach this simple experience, this prayer of the heart. Don't teach methods; don't teach some lofty way to pray. *Teach the prayer of God's Spirit,* not of man's invention.'[1]

The first way of coming into the Prayer of the Heart

is by simple love. Love is the response of the heart to the overwhelming goodness of God, so come in simply and speak to him in unvarnished honesty. You may be so awestruck and so full of love at his presence that words do not come. This is all right! It is enough to experience what Brennan Manning calls 'the wisdom of accepted tenderness'.[2]

You may be given a special love name for God that you can breathe quietly over and over as often as necessary to call you back into his loving presence. Such a love name could be simply, 'Abba, Father' or you might use Spurgeon's favourite name for God, taken from the Song of Solomon: 'My Well Beloved'.

If you have disturbing thoughts, simply return to your special name for God, and the distractions will be driven out. If you must do this fifty times in an hour, you have made fifty beautiful acts of love towards God.

Speak words of love and compassion to the Father. It may feel strange and unnatural at first, for you are not used to loving God. However, in time you will find that love language is perfectly natural to those who are in love.

Falling asleep in prayer is no problem. You can rest in God's presence. Besides, to be next to the heart of God is a good place, a safe place, for sleeping. The anonymous author of *The Cloud of Unknowing* says to thank God if in prayer you fall asleep unawares.[3]

The prayer 'Abba, I belong to you' is a perfect body rhythm prayer. It contains seven syllables that can be spoken easily in one breath. You will be led to other similar prayers.

We are, of course, commanded to love God with all our heart, soul, mind and strength. But you may find it difficult to love God. Every effort seems to leave you cold and hard of heart. You are not moved by God's grace and mercy. You are left untouched by his love and care. What are you to do?

I suggest that you begin by inviting God to kindle a fire of love within you. Ask him to develop an ache in your heart. Then when you are outside of his nearness for any length of time, this ache will begin again in you and will draw you back to his loving presence.

But even this may not be strong enough medicine for you. Is there anything left to do? Yes, indeed! I commend to you the prayer of John Donne 'Batter my heart, three-personed God.'[4] This is the first line of a sonnet in which Donne is describing how the goodness and gentleness of God failed to move him to repentance. He pleads with God to use strong-arm tactics to bring him round: 'Bend your force to break, blow, burn, and make me new.' It is a strong prayer, to be sure, but one that can have startling results.

Prayer

Reflection

There are several different ways of coming into the Prayer of the Heart mentioned in the passage above. Choose the prayer that is most appropriate for you at present.

Come before God and express your love to him in silence, or choose a simple prayer such as 'Abba I belong to you' and repeat it with each breath.

Ask God to kindle a fire of love within you, an ache in your heart that can only be satisfied by his presence.

Use the prayer of John Donne: 'Bend your force, to break, blow, burn and make me new'; or else put the strength of his sentiment into words of your own.

SECTION 3

Moving Outward

Transformation and intimacy both cry out for ministry. We are led through the furnace of God's purity not just for our own sake but also for the sake of others. We are drawn up into the bosom of God's love not merely to experience unconditional acceptance for ourselves, but also so that we can give it to others.

The readings in this section call us into ministry to others. Love of God, of necessity, leads to love of neighbour. A life with God is inseparably linked to a concern for the poor and defenceless, and, like the Samaritan, we soon discover that our path often leads to the bleeding and broken of humanity.

21

Identification with the poor

Reading: Amos 5:10-15

*You hate the one who reproves in court
and despise him who tells the truth.*

*You trample on the poor
and force him to give you grain.
Therefore, though you have built stone mansions,
you will not live in them;
though you have planted lush vineyards,
you will not drink their wine.
For I know how many are your offences
and how great your sins.*

*You oppress the righteous and take bribes
and you deprive the poor of justice in the courts.
Therefore the prudent man keeps quiet in such times,
for the times are evil.*

*Seek good, not evil,
that you may live.
Then the Lord God Almighty will be with you,
just as you say he is.
Hate evil, love good;
maintain justice in the courts.
Perhaps the Lord God Almighty will have mercy
on the remnant of Joseph.*

Another way in which simplicity takes outward shape is through conscious identification with the poor and forgotten. Jesus Christ did so repeatedly, and so must we. The exact expression of our identification will have infinite variety, but there is no doubt that we ought to engage in this loving work.

Many of us need to champion the cause of the oppressed, witness to their misery, and call for justice. We are to plead their cause before the powerful. The Christian is to be the voice of the voiceless, the face of the faceless, before authorities. Is this not precisely what Moses did before Pharaoh? When we represent the poor before the powerful, we are ambassadors of Christ. Quakers on the American frontier would often attend treaty negotiations between the federal government and the Indian tribes in order to plead for justice. Jacques Ellul says, 'I hold that in every situation of injustice and oppression, the Christian – who cannot deal with it by violence – must make himself completely a part of it as representative of the victims.'[1]

But a warning is needed here. The Christian must advocate the cause of those who are truly poor and forgotten. So often it seems as if Christians have a particular knack for joining causes that are nearly over and championing issues that have thousands of champions. We must go beyond newspaper accounts (in fact, newspapers are usually a hindrance in this work) to find the genuinely dispossessed. If we desire to identify with the poor we will be concerned to be informed, really informed. Ellul reminds us that Christians 'must be so concerned about human misery that they take pains to discover the really lost before it is too late.'[2]

This is a thankless ministry. We are seeking to be led by the Holy Spirit to the truly abandoned and defenceless. We will defend the cause of people who are not politically 'interesting'. We will be bringing before mayors and councillors issues that all others would like to sweep under the rug. We will be making people uncomfortable over matters they deem 'trivial'. But that is what is asked of us if we are to identify with the genuinely poor and forgotten.

Another way we identify with the poor is to be among them. There are some who are led to take this up as a vocation: living among the poor, suffering with the poor, praying for the poor. Albert Schweitzer lived this vocation in Africa as did Toyohiko Kagawa in Japan.

Many of us, however, will be called to be among the abandoned of the earth in less dramatic ways. We will respond to Divine promptings to visit prisons and hospitals, rest homes and mental institutions. We will tutor little ones deprived of basic skills. We will take time to play with the child down the street that sits on the kerb alone.

Our children need to join us in this ministry of identification. We do them no favour by hiding them from suffering and need. If we imprison them in ghettos of affluence, how can they learn compassion for the broken of the world? So, let us walk hand in hand with our children into pockets of misery and suffering.

One specific means of identification with the poor is discovered in our approach to education. Do we see a college education, for example, as a ticket to privilege or as a training for service to the needy? What do we teach our teenagers in this matter? Do we urge them to enter college because it will better equip them to serve? Or do we try to bribe them with promises of future status and salary increases? No wonder they graduate more deeply concerned about their standard of living then about suffering humanity.

As we seek to follow in the steps of Jesus, we will be drawn to identify with the poor. As we do, perhaps a valuable question to keep before us is whether we are as willing to evaluate our living standards by the needs of the poor as we are by the lifestyle of our neighbours.

Freedom of Simplicity

Reflection

Often the poor remain hidden from us, even when we benefit from their labour. How can those who labour on your behalf become more visible to you?

For one month shop in poorer neighbourhoods and see what you learn.

Are there spheres of influence where you can be a voice for the voiceless?

22

Diary of a confession

Reading: James 5:13–16

*Are any among you suffering? They should pray. Are
any cheerful? They should sing songs of praise. Are
any among you sick? They should call for the elders
of the church and have them pray over them, anointing
them with oil in the name of the Lord. The prayer
of faith will save the sick, and the Lord will raise
them up; and anyone who has committed sins will be
forgiven. Therefore confess your sins to one another,
and pray for one another, so that you may be healed.
The prayer of the righteous is powerful and effective*
(NRSV).

Although I had read in the Bible about the ministry
of confession in the Christian fellowship, I had never
experienced it until I was pastoring my first church. I
did not take the difficult step of laying bare my inner
life to another out of any deep burden or sense of sin.
I did not feel there was anything wrong in the least –
except one thing. I longed for more power to do the
work of God. I felt inadequate to deal with many of

the desperate needs that confronted me. There had to be more spiritual resources than I was experiencing (and I'd had all the Holy Spirit experiences you're supposed to have; you name them, I'd had them!). 'Lord,' I prayed, 'is there more you want to bring into my life? I want to be conquered and ruled by you. If there is anything blocking thc flow of your power, reveal it to me.' He did. Not by an audible voice or even through any human voice, but simply by a growing impression that perhaps something in my past was impeding the flow of his life. So I devised a plan. I divided my life into three periods: childhood, adolescence, adulthood. On the first day I came before God in prayer and meditation, pencil and paper in hand. Inviting him to reveal to me anything during my childhood that needed either forgiveness or healing or both, I waited in absolute silence for some ten minutes. Anything about my childhood that surfaced to my conscious mind, I wrote down. I made no attempt to analyse the items or put any value judgment on them. My assurance was that God would reveal anything that needed his healing touch. Having finished, I put the pencil and paper down for the day. The next day I went through the same exercise for my adolescent years, and the third day for my adult years.

Paper in hand, I then went to a dear brother in Christ. I had made arrangements with him a week ahead so he understood the purpose of our meeting. Slowly, sometimes painfully, I read my sheet, adding only those comments necessary to make the sin clear. When I had finished, I began to return the paper to my briefcase. Wisely, my counsellor/confessor gently stopped my hand and took the sheet of paper. Without a word he took a wastebasket, and, as I watched, he tore the paper into hundreds of tiny pieces and dropped them into it. That powerful, non-verbal expression of forgiveness was followed by a simple absolution. My sins, I knew, were as far away as the east is from the west.

Next, my friend, with the laying on of hands, prayed a

prayer of healing for all the sorrows and hurts of the past. The power of that prayer lives with me today.

I cannot say I experienced any dramatic feelings: I did not. In fact, the entire experience was an act of sheer obedience with no compelling feelings in the least. But I am convinced that it set me free in ways I had not known before. It seemed that I was released to explore what were for me new and uncharted regions of the Spirit.

Celebration of Discipline

Reflection

Why do you think the ministry of confession to a brother or sister in Christ is so seldom exercised in our day? What are its values as against private confession?

Examine your own life before God for five minutes in silence. Is there anything he is asking you to confess? (If nothing is revealed to you, then do not try to unearth something from your subconscious.) If God brings something to mind, then confess the sin to him and ask his forgiveness. If you do not feel sure that you are forgiven, then it may be an occasion to seek out another Christian in whom you can confide and make your confession to him or her.

23

Forgiveness without pretending

Reading: Matthew 18:15–18

*'If another member of the church sins against you, go
and point out the fault when the two of you are alone. If
the member listens to you, you have regained that one.
But if you are not listened to, take one or two others
along with you, so that every word may be confirmed
by the evidence of two or three witnesses. If the member
refuses to listen to them, tell it to the church; and if the
offender refuses to listen even to the church, let such a
one be to you as a Gentile and a tax collector. Truly I
tell you, whatever you bind on earth will be bound in
heaven, and whatever you loose on earth will be loosed
in heaven* (NRSV).

Confession is a corporate discipline because sin both
offends God and creates a wound in the Christian fellowship. In the early centuries of the Christian era forgiveness
and reconciliation involved a lengthy process of healing
by which the offender was restored to health through the
ministry of the total Christian community. In the early
Middle Ages it was turned increasingly into a private

sacrament, and following the Reformation Protestants began to view it more and more as a matter exclusively between the individual and God. But in the beginning, confession was not the privatistic event it is today; in fact, in Matthew 18 Jesus expressed its essential communal nature and explained how forgiveness can come into the community without destroying it. It is God who does the forgiving, but often he chooses human beings as the channel of his forgiving grace.

Human beings are such that 'life together' always involves them in hurting one another in some way. And forgiveness is essential in a community of hurt and hurtful persons. In experiencing forgiveness it is important to understand what it is *not*. For things are often mistaken for forgiveness.

First, some imagine forgiveness means a pretending that it doesn't really matter. 'Oh, that's all right, it really didn't hurt me anyway!' we say. That is not forgiveness; it is lying. And love and lies do not mix well. The truth is that these things matter a great deal, and it does not help to avoid the issue. What we need is not avoidance but reconciliation.

Second, some think that forgiveness means a ceasing to hurt. There is the belief that if we continue to hurt, we must have failed to truly forgive. That is simply not true. Hurting is not evil. We may hurt for a very long time to come. Forgiveness does not mean that we will stop hurting.

Third, many would have us believe that forgiveness means forgetting. 'Forgive and forget', as we often say. But the truth of the matter is that we cannot forget. We remember; the difference will be that we no longer need or desire to use the memory against others. The memory remains, the vindictiveness leaves. The attempt to force people to forget what cannot be forgotten only puts them in bondage and confuses the meaning of forgiveness.

Fourth, many assume that to forgive means to pretend

that the relationship is just the same as before the offence. But this is simply not the case. The relationship will never be the same again. We might just as well make peace with that *fact*. By the grace of God it may be a hundred times better, but it will never be the same.

True confession and forgiveness brings joy to the Christian community and healing to the parties involved. Most wonderful of all it spells reconciliation with God the Father, for as the beloved apostle said so long ago, 'If we confess our sins, he is faithful and just, and will forgive our sins and cleanse us from all unrighteousness' (I John 1:9 RSV).

Celebration of Discipline

Reflection
What are the four things that fogiveness is *not?* Are any of them autobiographical?

Think of a situation where you need to forgive someone. It may be a longstanding grievance in a relationship or a relatively minor irritation that happened this week. Remind yourself what you are not attempting to do in forgiving that person. Then ask God to help you release the situation in true forgiveness.

For further study: What is our assurance of forgiveness? See I John 1:5–10

24

Praying the ordinary

Reading: Genesis 2:4b–9, 15

*When the Lord God made the earth and the heavens –
and no shrub of the field had yet appeared on the earth
and no plant of the field had yet sprung up, for the Lord
God had not sent rain on the earth and there was no man
to work the ground, but streams came up from the earth
and watered the whole surface of the ground – the Lord
God formed the man from the dust of the ground and
breathed into his nostrils the breath of life, and the man
became a living being.*

*Now the Lord God had planted a garden in the east,
in Eden; and there he put the man he had formed. And
the Lord God made all kinds of trees grow out of the
ground – trees that were pleasing to the eye and good
for food. In the middle of the garden were the tree of
life and the tree of the knowledge of good and evil.*

*The Lord God took the man and put him in the
Garden of Eden to work it and take care of it.*

'Whether you eat or drink, or whatever you do, do
everything for the glory of God' is St Paul's counsel

(I Cor. 10:31 NRSV). I came into a fuller understanding of this counsel when, as a teenager, I was privileged to spend a summer among the Eskimo people of Kotzebue, Alaska. The Eskimo Christians I met there had a deep sense of the wholeness of life with no break between their prayer and their work.

I had come to Kotzebue on the adventure of helping to 'build the first high school above the Arctic Circle', but the work itself was far from an adventure. It was hard, backbreaking labour. One day I was trying to dig a trench for a sewer line – no small task in a world of frozen tundra. An Eskimo man whose face and hands displayed the leathery toughness of many winters came by and watched me for a while. Finally he said simply and profoundly, 'You are digging a ditch to the glory of God.' He said it to encourage me, I know. And I have never forgotten his words. Beyond my Eskimo friend no human being ever knew or cared whether I dug that ditch well or poorly. In time it was to be covered up and forgotten. But because of my friend's words, I dug with all my might, for every shovelful of dirt was a prayer to God. Even though I did not know it at the time, I was attempting in my small and unsophisticated way to do what the great artisans of the Middle Ages did when they carved the back of a piece of art, knowing that God alone would see it.

Anthony Bloom writes, 'A prayer makes sense only if it is lived. Unless they are "lived", unless life and prayer become completely interwoven, prayers become a sort of polite madrigal which you offer to God at moments when you are giving time to him.'[1] The work of our hands and of our minds is acted-out prayer, a love offering to the living God. In what is perhaps the finest line in the movie *Chariots of Fire,* Olympic runner Eric Liddell tells his sister, 'Jenny, when I run, I feel his pleasure.' This is the reality that is to permeate all vocations whether we are writing a novel or cleaning a latrine.

It is at the latrine cleaning that many have a problem. It is not hard to see how a Michelangelo or a T. S. Eliot is giving glory to God – theirs are creative vocations. But what about the boring jobs, the unimportant jobs, the mundane jobs. How are those prayer?

Here we must understand the order in the kingdom of God. It is precisely in the 'slop-bucket job' – the work that we abhor – where we will find God the most. We do not need to have good feelings or a warm glow in order to do work for the glory of God. All good work is pleasing to the Father. Even the jobs that seem meaningless and mindless to us are highly valued in the order of the kingdom of God. God values the ordinary.

Prayer

Reflection
Do you see your work as a hindrance to prayer or as prayer itself?

Praying, eating breakfast, doing the washing-up, driving to work, playing snooker, going to church . . . which of these activities are 'spiritual'? How might it be possible to do each of them to the glory of God?

Can a person glorify God without working?

25

A Spirit-led people

Reading: Acts 13:1-3

In the church at Antioch there were prophets and teachers: Barnabas, Simeon called Niger, Lucius of Cyrene, Manaen (who had been brought up with Herod the tetrarch) and Saul. While they were worshipping the Lord and fasting, the Holy Spirit said, 'Set apart for me Barnabas and Saul for the work to which I have called them.' So after they had fasted and prayed, they placed their hands on them and sent them off.

In our day heaven and earth are on tiptoe waiting for the emergence of a Spirit-led, Spirit-intoxicated, Spirit-empowered people. All of creation watches expectantly for the springing up of a disciplined, freely gathered, martyr people who know in this life the life and power of the kingdom of God. It has happened before. It can happen again.

Indeed, in movements all over the world we are now beginning to see the breaking forth of the apostolic church of the Spirit. Many are having a deep and profound experience of an Emmanuel of the Spirit – God with us; a knowledge that in the power of the Spirit Jesus has come to guide his people himself; an experience of his leading that is as definite and as immediate as the cloud by day and the pillar of fire by night.

But the knowledge of the direct, active, immediate leading of the Spirit is not sufficient. Individual guidance must yield to corporate guidance. There must also come a knowledge of the direct, active, immediate leading of the Spirit *together*. I do not mean 'corporate guidance' in an organisational sense, but in an organic and functional sense. Church councils and denominational decrees are simply not of this reality.

One of the most delightful examples comes from 'the poor little monk of Assisi', St Francis. Francis, it seems, was in 'great agony of doubt' about whether he should devote himself only to prayer and meditation, which was a common practice in those days, or whether he should also engage in preaching missions. Wisely, Francis sought out counsel. 'As the holy humility that was in him did not allow him to trust in himself or in his own prayers, he humbly turned to others in order to know God's will in this matter.'

He sent messages to two of his most trusted friends, Sister Clare and Brother Silvester, asking them to meet with one of their 'purer and more spiritual companions' and seek the will of God in the matter. Immediately, they gathered to pray and both Sister Clare and Brother Silvester returned with the same answer.

When the messenger returned, St Francis first washed his feet and prepared him a meal. Then, kneeling down before the messenger, St Francis asked him, 'What does my Lord Jesus Christ order me to do?' The messenger replied that Christ had revealed that 'He wants you to go about the world preaching, because God did not call you for yourself alone but also for the salvation of others.' Receiving the message as the undisputed word of Christ, St Francis jumped up saying, 'So let's go – in the name of the Lord', whereupon he immediately embarked on a preaching mission. That direction gave the early Franciscan movement an unusual combination of mystical contemplation and evangelistic fervour.

In this experience Francis was doing more than seeking out the advice of wise counsellors. He was seeking a way to open the windows of heaven to reveal the mind of Christ, and he took it as such – to the great good of all to whom he ministered.

Celebration of Discipline

Reflection
What are the difficulties and advantages of corporate guidance as opposed to individuals seeking God's will?

Are our church meetings and committees a true expression of being led by the Spirit? On what basis are our decisions usually made?

How could we begin to practise Spirit-led guidance in our homes, business or church?

For further study: Read the first half of the Book of Acts (chapters 1–15) noting the central role corporate guidance played in the growth of the early church.

26

Sexuality – male and female

Reading: Genesis 1:26–8

Then God said, 'Let us make man in our image, in our likeness, and let them rule over the fish of the sea and the birds of the air, over the livestock, over all the earth, and over all the creatures that move along the ground.'

So God created man
in his own image,
in the image of God
he created him;
male and female
he created them.

God blessed them and said to them, 'Be fruitful and increase in number; fill the earth and subdue it. Rule over the fish of the sea and the birds of the air and over every living creature that moves on the ground.'

In the first chapter of Genesis we have a brief, yet magnificent, comment on the meaning of human sexuality. The narrative opens in majesty as God brings the universe into existence by speaking the creative word. And this universe that he created is good, very good. (Please, let us get it straight once and for all: the material world is good and not to be despised. We urgently need to recover a doctrine of God as Creator and of a creation that is good, very good.)

Human beings are the apex of God's creation. In simple, yet noble, language we are told that the human creation is set apart from all others, for it is in the *imago Dei*, the image of God. Notice how closely related our human sexuality is to the *imago Dei*: 'So God created man in his own image, in the image of God he created him; *male and female he created them*' (Gen. 1:27 RSV, emphasis mine). Strange as it may seem, our sexuality, our maleness and femaleness, is somehow related to our creation in the image of God.

Karl Barth was the first major theologian to help us see the implications of this tremendous confession of scripture that human sexuality is grounded in the *imago Dei*. What he has helped us understand is that relationship is at the heart of what it means to be 'in the image of God' and that the relationship between male and female is the human expression of our relationship with God.

Our human sexuality, our maleness and femaleness, is not just an accidental arrangement of the human species, not just a conventional way to keep the human race going. No, it is at the centre of our true humanity. We exist as male and female in relationship. Our sexualness, our capacity to love and be loved, is intimately related to our creation in the image of God. What a high view of human sexuality!

Notice too that the biblical stress upon relationship helps to enlarge our understanding of human sexuality. The problem with the topless bars and the pornographic literature of our day is not that they emphasise sexuality too much but that they do not emphasise it enough. They totally eliminate relationship and restrain sexuality to the narrow confines of the genital. They have made sex trivial.

How much richer and fuller is the biblical perspective. To chat over coffee, to discuss a great book, to view a sunset together – this is sexuality at its best, for male and female are in intimate relationship. To be sure, genital sex is a part of the total picture, but human sexuality is a far larger reality than merely coitus.

Money

Reflection
The Christian view of sexuality is often perceived as disapproving and restrictive. How would you attempt to convince a friend that Christians in fact have a higher view of sexuality?

Why has sex in our own age become so associated with secrecy and forbidden pleasure? What has happened to human sexuality since the fall when the man and woman were 'naked and not ashamed'?

For further study: Read the Song of Songs for an unashamed celebration of sensuality and sexuality in the Bible. What does this book say about God's view of sex and sexuality?

27

The grace of giving

Reading: Isaiah 58:5–8

Is this the kind of fast I have chosen,
only a day for a man to humble himself?
Is it only for bowing one's head like a reed
and for lying on sackcloth and ashes?
Is that what you call a fast,
a day acceptable to the Lord?

Is not this the kind of fasting I have chosen:
to loose the chains of injustice
and untie the cords of the yoke,
to set the oppressed free
and break every yoke?
Is it not to share your food with the hungry
and to provide the poor wanderer with shelter –
when you see the naked, to clothe him,
and not to turn away from your own flesh and blood?
Then your light will break forth like the dawn,
and your healing will quickly appear;
then your righteousness will go before you,
and the glory of the Lord will be your rear guard.

The grace of giving is often a tremendous stimulant to the life of faith. This is why the offering is correctly placed as part of the worship experience.

In Isaiah 58 we read of a very religious people whose pious devotion counted for nothing because it was not matched with active caring for the poor and the oppressed. 'Is not this the fast that I choose', proclaims God, 'to loose the bonds of wickedness, to undo the thongs of the yoke, to let the oppressed go free, and to break every yoke?' (Isa. 58:6 RSV). Religious piety is bankrupt without justice. If you want your fasting to have true spiritual content, then you are to 'share your bread with the hungry, and bring the homeless poor into your house' (Isa. 58:7 RSV).

If our spiritual vitality seems low, if Bible study produces only dusty words, if prayer seems hollow and empty, then perhaps a prescription of lavish and joyful giving is just what we need. Giving brings authenticity and vitality to our devotional experience.

Money is an effective way of showing our love to God because it is so much a part of us. One economist put it this way: 'Money as a form of power is so intimately related to the possessor that one cannot consistently give money without giving self.'[1] In a sense, money is coined personality, so tied to who we are that when we give it we are giving ourselves. We sing, 'Take my life and let it be, consecrated, Lord, to Thee.' But we must flesh out that consecration in specific ways, which is why the next line of the hymn says, 'Take my silver and my gold, not a mite would I withhold.' We consecrate ourselves by consecrating our money.

Dr Karl Menninger once asked one wealthy patient, 'What on earth are you going to do with all that money?' The patient replied, 'Just worry about it, I suppose!' Dr Menninger went on, 'Well, do you get that much pleasure out of worrying about it?' 'No,' responded the patient, 'but I get such terror when I think of giving some of it to somebody.'[2]

Now, this 'terror' is real. When we let go of money we are letting go of part of ourselves and part of our security. But this is precisely why it is important to do it. It is one way to obey Jesus' command to deny ourselves. 'If any man would come after me, let him deny himself and take up his cross daily and follow me' (Luke 9:23 RSV).

When we give money we are releasing a little more of our egocentric selves and a little more of our false security. John Wesley declared that 'if you have any desire to escape the damnation of hell, give us all you can; otherwise I can have no more hope of your salvation than that of Judas Iscariot.'[3]

Giving frees us from the tyranny of money. But we do not just give money; we give the things money has purchased. In Acts the early Christian community gave houses and land to provide funds for those in need (Acts 4:32–7). Have you ever considered selling a car or a stamp collection to help finance someone's education? Money has also given us the time and leisure to acquire skills. What about giving those skills away? Doctors, dentists, lawyers, computer experts, and many others can give their skills for the good of the community.

Giving frees us to care. It produces an air of expectancy as we anticipate what God will lead us to give. It makes life with God an adventure of discovery. We are being used to help make a difference in the world, and that is worth living for and giving for.[4]

Money

Reflection

In what sense is it true that 'one cannot consistently give money without giving self'?

What kind of feelings does the prospect of giving away money evoke in you? In what fears or experiences are these feelings rooted?

Review your own giving before God – not only in monetary terms but counting your skills and possessions. One method is to use pen and paper to list what you have to give; then ask God what he is leading you to use for the benefit of others.

28

Spiritual power

Reading: 1 Corinthians 13:1–7

If I speak in the tongues of men and of angels, but have not love, I am only a resounding gong or a clanging cymbal. If I have the gift of prophecy and can fathom all mysteries and all knowledge, and if I have a faith that can move mountains, but have not love, I am nothing. If I give all I possess to the poor and surrender my body to the flames, but have not love, I gain nothing.

Love is patient, love is kind. It does not envy, it does not boast, it is not proud. It is not rude, it is not self-seeking, it is not easily angered, it keeps no record of wrongs. Love does not delight in evil but rejoices with the truth. It always protects, always trusts, always hopes, always perseveres.

The power that creates is spiritual power, and it is in stark contrast to human power. The Apostle Paul spoke of the 'flesh', and by it he meant human-initiated activity without the aid of divine grace. People can do many things in the power of the flesh, but they cannot do the work of the Spirit of God. The power of the flesh relies upon such things as proper pedigree, positions of status, and connections among those in the power structure. But Paul, you see, had given up on the flesh. He said that he counted those things as 'dung', for his sights were set on a greater power, 'that I may know him and the power of his resurrection, and may share his sufferings, becoming like him in his death, that if possible I may attain the resurrection from the dead' (Phil. 3:10–11 RSV).

Now, when we see people desperately scrambling for the 'dung' – human power – we can be sure that they know precious little of the 'power of his resurrection'. What, then, are the marks of this power that proceeds from God?

Love is the first mark of spiritual power. Love demands that power be used for the good of others. Notice Jesus' use of power – the healing of the blind, the sick, the maimed, the dumb, the leper and many others. Luke, the physician, observes that 'all the crowd sought to touch him, for power came forth from him and healed them all' (Luke 6:19 RSV). Notice in each case the concern for the good of others, the motivation of love. In Christ, power is used to destroy the evil so that love can redeem the good.

Power for the purpose of advancing reputations or inflating egos is not power motivated by love. When God used Paul and Barnabas to heal a cripple at Lystra, the astonished people tried to turn them into Greek gods, but they tore their clothes and shouted out, 'We also are men, of like nature with you' (Acts 14:15 RSV). Many of us might not find the idea of deity status so reprehensible. Think of the power over people we would have, and, after all, we would use the power to such good ends! But power that is used to advance reputations destroys the user, because with it we aspire to be gods.

This leads us to the second mark of spiritual power, humility. Humility is power under control. Nothing is more dangerous than power in the service of arrogance. Power under the discipline of humility is teachable. Apollos was a powerful preacher, but he was also willing to learn from others (Acts 18:24–6). In the course of his powerful ministry, Peter made some serious mistakes, but when confronted with his errors he had the humility to change (e.g., Acts 10:1–35; Gal. 2:11–21).

Believe me, this is no small matter. Many have been destroyed in their walk with God simply because their exercise of power was not controlled by humility. Power without humility is anything but a blessing.

Money

Reflection

You may think of yourself as someone for whom power is not a big issue. Ask yourself in what capacity do you exercise power (however limited) and over which people? In the family? As a parent? Or as a son or daughter? As a friend? At work? In your church? In any other positions you hold in the community?

Re-read the famous passage about love in I Corinthians 13. Use it as a yardstick for the way you exercise power in any of the above areas. Are you patient? Kind? Without envy, pride or boasting?

For further study: Read the account of Saul's jealousy of David in I Samuel, which illustrates how the desire to hold on to power can corrupt and destroy relationships.

29

What is our world like?

Reading: John 3:16–21

'For God so loved the world that he gave his one and only son, that whoever believes in him shall not perish but have eternal life. For God did not send his Son into the world to condemn the world, but to save the world through him.

Whoever believes in him is not condemned, but whoever does not believe stands condemned already because he has not believed in the name of God's one and only Son. This is the verdict: Light has come into the world, but men loved darkness instead of light because their deeds were evil. Everyone who does evil hates the light, and will not come into the light for fear that his deeds will be exposed. But whoever lives by the truth comes into the light, so that it may be seen plainly that what he has done has been done through God.'

As we face the close of the twentieth century, we need the courage to see the world as it truly is. Many lack this courage. An educated and prosperous professional woman articulated the feelings of vast numbers, 'Global consciousness is what I really hate . . . It is spoiling my life. I can't stand to have all those pictures of misery, violence and injustice in the world dumped into my living room through the TV.'[1] At times we all feel that way. We are overwhelmed by the immensity of the problem and feel helpless to respond.

But we must never succumb to the temptation to self-centred provincialism. We dare not close our eyes to world events by relegating them into neatly packaged eschatological schemes that relieve us of any responsibility. We dare not stop our ears to the sobbing moan of the world's hungry by the insulated assertion that these things must occur before the return of Christ. May God give us eyes to see and ears to hear the world in which we live.

What is our world like? Three billion people have yet to hear the redemption that is in Jesus Christ. Nearly two and one-half billion are culturally outside the present scope of Christian witness. They die without hearing, without knowing. Business as usual will never accomplish the great irrevocable mandate to world evangelisation.

What is our world like? We are split between the fat, prosperous affluent and the weak, hungry poor. The gap is widening with alarming speed. Two-thirds of the world, over one hundred nations, suffer chronic food deficiencies while a handful of wealthy nations have attained the highest peaks of material abundance known in the history of humankind.

What is our world like? Nations are irreversibly interdependent. The United States now imports nearly 50 per cent of its vital resources, and exports vast amounts of food and technology. Any national decision anywhere sends repercussions throughout the globe. Ready or not, like it or not, we are a married world with no divorce possible.

What is our world like? Our planet is plagued by overpopulation and over-consumption. The net increase in world population now stands at about two hundred thousand a day or seventy-three million per year. No one knows the carrying capacity of our globe but it is likely that we are pushing the limits. Overpopulation is the problem of the third and fourth world; over-consumption is the West. The average American child this year will consume as much of the world's resources as twenty children born in India. Deliberate and calculated waste is the central aspect of the Western economy. We over-eat, over-buy, and over-build, spewing out our toxic wastes upon the earth and into the air.

But this gloomy picture is not the final word. Hope has the final word. We are not locked into a prison of determinism: change is possible. Ruthless inequities can be eradicated. The hungry can be fed. Millions can be reached with the message of life in Christ. He whose power is over all desires to use his people as agents of change. We are to walk cheerfully over the face of the earth, conquering evil with good in the power of the Spirit.

Freedom of Simplicity

Reflection

Use your prayers today to face the world we live in and bring its pain, injustice and suffering before our Maker. Spread out the double page of a newspaper on the floor (preferably one that deals with world events) and use it as a focus for your prayers. (If you don't have a recent newspaper, use a television or radio news bulletin as your mental focus). Hold each event before God in silence, asking him to show you the spiritual and moral reality behind the news stories, the institutions and the politics. Finally, ask God how you can pray for hope and change in these situations.

Persisting in prayer

Reading: Luke 18:1–8

Then Jesus told his disciples a parable to show them that they should always pray and not give up. He said: 'In a certain town there was a judge who neither feared God nor cared about men. And there was a widow in that town who kept coming to him with the plea, "Grant me justice against my adversary." '

'For some time he refused. But finally he said to himself, "Even though I don't fear God or care about men, yet because this widow keeps bothering me, I will see that she gets justice, so that she won't eventually wear me out with her coming!"

And the Lord said, 'Listen to what the unjust judge says. And will not God bring about justice for his chosen ones, who cry out to him day and night? Will he keep putting them off? I tell you, he will see that they get justice, and quickly. However, when the Son of Man comes, will he find faith on the earth?'

When we begin praying for others, we soon discover that it is easy to become discouraged at the results which seem frustratingly slow and uneven. This is because we are entering the strange mix of divine influence and human autonomy. God never compels, and so the divine influence always allows a way of escape. No one is ever forced into a robot style of obedience.

This aspect of God's character – this respect, this courtesy, this patience – is hard for us to accept because we operate so differently. Some people frustrate us so much that sometimes we wish we could open up their heads and tinker around inside a bit. This is our way, but it is not God's way. His way is higher than our way. His way is like the rain and the snow that gently fall to the earth, disappearing into the ground as they nourish it. When the time is right, up springs new life. No manipulation, no control; perfect freedom, perfect liberty. This is God's way (Isa. 55:8–11).

This process is a hard one for us to accept, and we can easily become disheartened by it. I think Jesus understood this, and, as a result, he gave more than one teaching on our need for persistence – what we today call the parables of importunity. He even specifies his reason for telling these stories, namely that we would 'pray always and not . . . lose heart' (Luke 18:1 RSV).

These parables have been a special grace to me, for how quickly I lose heart. Perhaps you know what I mean. We pray once or twice, and when nothing seems to move, we go on to other matters, or sulk in self-pity, or even give up on prayer altogether. Our quick-fix approach is a little like turning on a light switch, and, if the lights do not come on immediately, declaring, 'Well, I didn't believe in electricity anyway!'

But Jesus gives us an altogether different vantage point from which to view our prayer work. Prayer, he says, is a little like a helpless widow who refuses to accept her helplessness and instead stands up to injustice, and her persistence wins the day. It is something like forcing a neighbour to help provide food for a stranger – even though to do so is terribly inconvenient – because otherwise the whole village will be disgraced for not caring for the stranger in their midst (Luke 11:5–13). In each case the point of the teaching is persistence. We keep asking, we keep seeking, we keep knocking.

There is a religious word for what I have been describing: supplication. Supplication means to ask with earnestness, with intensity, with perseverance. It is a declaration that we are deadly serious about this prayer business. We are going to keep at it and not give up. John Calvin writes, 'We must repeat the same supplications not twice or three times only, but as often as we have need, a hundred and a thousand times . . . We must never be weary in waiting for God's help.'[1]

Prayer

Reflection
Look back on what God has taught you over the past weeks. Use your spiritual journal if you have been keeping one. You may like to use the following questions as a framework for your review:

1. What have I learnt or experienced in a new way?

2. What do I want to thank God for?

3. What resolve do I want to make, with God's help, in relation to my future prayer life?

Notes

Chapter 1
1. Emilie Griffin, *Clinging: The Experience of Prayer* (San Francisco: Harper & Row, 1984), p. 5.

Chapter 2
1. C. S. Lewis, *Letters to Malcolm: Chiefly on Prayer* (New York: Harcourt, Brace & World, 1964), p. 98.
2. Phineas Fletcher, untitled poem from *Hail, Gladdening Light: Music of the English Church*, Cambridge Singers dir. John Rutter (UK: Collegium Records, COLCD 113, 1991) Stereo/digital compact disc.

Chapter 3
1. Catherine Marshall, *Beyond Our Selves* (New York: McGraw-Hill, 1961), p. 94.

Chapter 5
1. John Woolman, *The Journal of John Woolman* (Secaucus, NJ: Citadel, 1972), p. 11.

Chapter 6
1. Thomas Kelly, *A Testament of Devotion* (New York: Harper & Row, 1941), p. 53.

Chapter 7

1. Thomas Kelly, *A Testament of Devotion* (London: Quaker Home Service, 1979), p. 115.
2. Thomas Kelly, *A Testament of Devotion*, p. 115.
3. Thomas Kelly, *A Testament of Devotion*, p. 115.

Chapter 11

1. Thomas à Kempis, *The Imitation of Christ* (London: Hodder & Stoughton, 1979).

Chapter 12

1. Martin Buber, *Tales of the Hasidim: Early Masters* (New York: Schocken, 1948), p. 111.
2. André Gide, *If It Dies,* trans. Dorothy Bussey (New York: Random House, 1935), p. 83.
3. Evelyn Underhill, *Practical Mysticism* (New York: World, Meridian Books, 1955), pp. 93–94.
4. Fyodor Dostoevski, *The Brothers Karamazov* (London: Penguin, 1970).

Chapter 14

1. Francois Fénelon, *Christian Perfection* (Minneapolis: Bethany Fellowship, 1975), p. 4.

Chapter 15

1. Sue Monk Kidd, *God's Joyful Surprise* (San Francisco: Harper & Row, 1987), p. 200.

Chapter 16

1. Anthony Bloom, *Beginning to Pray* (New York: Paulist, 1970), pp. 92–94.

Chapter 17
1. P. T. Forsyth, *The Soul of Prayer* (Grand Rapids, MI: Eerdmans, 1916), p. 32.
2. Thomas Kelly, *A Testament of Devotion*, p. 45.
3. C. S. Lewis, *Letters to Malcolm: Chiefly on Prayer*, pp. 67–68.

Chapter 18
1. Thomas Kelly, *A Testament of Devotion*.

Chapter 19
1. Quoted in Edward W. Bauman, *Where Your Treasure Is* (Arlington, VA: Bauman Bible Telecasts, 1980), p. 73.

Chapter 20
1. Madame Guyon, *Experiencing the Depths of Jesus Christ* (Goleta, CA: Christian Books, 1975), p. 122.
2. See Brennan Manning, *The Wisdom of Accepted Tenderness*, (Denville, NJ: Dimension, 1978).
3. As noted in Mary Clare Vincent, *The Life of Prayer and the Way to God* (Still River, MS: St Bede's Publications, 1982), p. 81.
4. *The Complete Poems of John Donne*, ed. Walter Hendricks (Chicago: Packard, 1942), pp. 270–71.

Chapter 21
1. Jacques Ellul, *Violence: Reflections from a Christian Perspective* (Oxford: Mowbray, 1978).
2. Jacques Ellul, *Violence: Reflections from a Christian Perspective*.

Chapter 24

1. Anthony Bloom, *Beginning to Pray,* p. 59.

Chapter 27

1. Quoted in Bauman, *Where Your Treasure Is,* p. 113.
2. Quoted in Bauman, *Where Your Treasure Is,*
   pp. 89–90.
3. Quoted in Dallas Willard, "The Disciple's Solidarity
   with the Poor", 1984 (unpublished paper), p. 15.
4. I am indebted to Lynda Graybeal for this insight into
   the grace of giving.

Chapter 29

1. James Scherer, *Global Living Here and Now* (New
   York: Friendship, 1974), p. 6.

Chapter 30

1. John Calvin, *Sermons on the Epistle to the Ephesians*
   (Edinburgh: Banner of Truth Trust, 1975), p. 683.